One Word

contemporary writers on the words they love or loathe

edited by

Molly McQuade

Sarabande  Books
LOUISVILLE, KENTUCKY

FIRST EDITION

Managing Editor
Sarabande Books, Inc.
2234 Dundee Road, Suite 200
Louisville, KY 40205

Library of Congress Cataloging-in-Publication Data

One word : contemporary writers on the words they love or loathe / edited by Molly McQuade. — 1st ed.
　　p. cm.
Includes bibliographical references and index.
ISBN 978-1-932511-85-7 (pbk. : alk. paper)
1. Vocabulary. 2. English language–Usage. 3. English language–Lexicography. I. McQuade, Molly.
PE1449.O53 2010
428–dc22
　　　　　　　　　　　　　　　　　2010004306
ISBN-13: 978-1-932511-85-7

Cover and text design by Kirkby Gann Tittle.

Manufactured in Canada
This book is printed on acid-free paper

Sarabande Books is a nonprofit literary organization.

The Kentucky Arts Council, the state arts agency, supports Sarabande Books with state tax dollars and federal funding from the National Endowment for the Arts.

From this walled city come all the words in the world. They are grown in orchards and once a week a word-market is held where people come to buy the words they need and trade-in those they have not used. For people wishing to make up their own words, individual letters are also on sale. Visitors should know the taste of letters before they acquire any: *A* tastes very good, but *Z* on the other hand is dry and tastes of sawdust. *X* is like stale air, *I* is icy and refreshing, *C* crunchy and *P* full of pips. A French connoisseur has described some letters according to colour rather than taste: *A* black, *E* white, *I* red, *U* green and *O* blue.

—Norton Juster

The chief glory of every people arises from its authors.

—Samuel Johnson

CONTENTS

Foreword / *vii*

The Words

A   Joel Brouwer / *9*
Ammavide   Meena Alexander / *18*
Ardor   Laura Jacobs / *19*
As   Brenda Hillman / *20*
Baffle   Albert Mobilio / *23*
Bitchin'   Star Black / *26*
Blog   Katherine DeLorenzo / *27*
Careen   Karen Stolz / *30*
Colander   Lee Martin / *32*
Corn   Katherine Karlin / *43*
Crash   Dan Moyer / *47*
Dämmerung   Susan Bernofsky / *52*
Darb   Erin McGraw / *54*
Dassn't   Richard Terrill / *56*
Dehiscence   Forrest Gander / *60*
Dive   Peggy Shumaker / *62*
Doom   Molly McQuade / *65*
Echo   Rusty Morrison / *67*
Eek   Daina Lyn Galante / *72*
Eye   Katherine Vaz / *74*
Fact   Srikanth Reddy / *76*
Felt   Annie Finch / *77*
Fiasco   Wendy Rawlings / *78*
Filthy   Marilyn Krysl / *82*
Floccinaucinihilipilification   Siobhan Gordon / *89*
Florere   Vincent Katz / *91*
Forget   Mimi Schwartz / *97*
Gray   William Corbett / *103*
Half-light   Maggie Hivnor / *105*
Hope   John Rodriguez / *109*
H.O.T.T.   Rachel Toor / *112*
I   Cynthia Gaver / *119*
Ickybicky   Megan Kossiakoff / *122*
Interesting   Jayson Iwen / *123*

Invisible   Dan Machlin / *126*
Kankedort   Maureen N. McLane / *129*
Lasai   Elizabeth Macklin / *134*
Lilac   Joan Connor / *136*
Line   Eleanor Wilner / *142*
Midnight   Willett Thomas / *145*
Negligee   Jane Delury / *147*
Nut   Andrew Hudgins / *150*
Or   Eric Ormsby / *152*
Pants   Nathaniel Taylor / *155*
Personal   Priscilla Becker / *157*
Prefer   Mark Noonan / *162*
Quipu   Arthur Sze / *165*
Riff   Ted Anton / *168*
Six-pack   Thylias Moss / *170*
Solmizate   Cole Swensen / *191*
Still   Robert Mueller / *193*
Subitane   John Taggart / *195*
Sweet   April Bernard / *197*
Sweetie   Lawrence Raab / *199*
Thermostat   Michael Martone / *202*
Topsoil   Mary Swander / *204*
Umami   Yong-Woong Shin / *213*
Umunnem   Kelechi Okere / *217*
Unknowable   Jillian Dungan / *220*
Ur   Robin Hemley / *222*
Verb   Lia Purpura / *224*
Verse   Albert Goldbarth / *227*
Very   Brock Clarke / *234*
Warrant   Kathy Briccetti / *238*
Wool   Daisy Fried / *240*
Wrong   John Shoptaw / *242*

Afterword / *245*
Contributor Notes / *249*
Author Index / *259*
The Editor / *261*

FOREWORD | Molly McQuade

Before I was a person, I was a word, although I didn't know which word I was. Please don't ask me to define it now. Looking back, this is all so hard to recall.

Still, when I try to remember what word I was, another word will sometimes come to mind, nudging me a little closer to the first. Tonight, that very word is *fog*.

The arrival of the "fog" word is sensibly opportune. For I sit facing San Francisco Bay, and I am feeling logical. Even so, the exact words confronting me now are not fog, but "Hyde St. Pier."

Mounted on huge pilings, and lit up without apology or aesthetic justification, the three words painted on the sign resemble the sort of composition made famous by the artist Lawrence Weiner. He hoists words, summoned in large letters, where we don't expect to see them, and by freeing certain words from their usual contexts, he allows them to live on as visual, imagined beings. In some respects that is also what this book of ours is doing—both with one word at a time and as a whole with them all.

The book wants words. The words want you to read them. They seek to change you. It is simple.

❖

When I began inviting writers to write about a word that meant a lot to them, I wasn't sure that anyone besides myself would feel like doing it. Silly me.

As the book gathered, I found myself wishing for yet more reach and randomness from it: for words from languages other than English; slang; proper nouns; invented words or phrases; a fitting babble.

Can the words read us?

In this dictionary, anyway, can we be read *by* our words?

Who works for whom?

Who is the boss?

Anyhow, I wished for a babble befitting the speaker, the reader, and the writer, who could say of themselves that each had lived at least one life as a word.

A | Joel Brouwer

A selects one but implies many, and so casts a pall of anxiety over its noun. "I'm not sure I want a relationship," she says, and immediately I imagine her turning the pages of a gigantic catalog of relationships, debating which, if any, she might want.

❖

A is a wager, a leap of faith, "a joyous shot at how things ought to be," as Philip Larkin wrote in his poem "Home Is So Sad." "Sad" because the shot, Larkin's quick to remind us, so often falls wide. But *A* doesn't know that. It can't, because at the moment a joyous shot becomes the shot that fell wide, *A*'s already moved on.

A's irrepressible. *A* never looks back.

A opens a restaurant, marries a sweetheart, places a bid, agrees to an experimental treatment. It's true that *A* never sticks around to see how the roll of the dice comes out, and

9

maybe that makes *A* irresponsible, but at least *A* takes a crack at it. Say what you will, but *A*'s an optimist.

❖

After *A* has seduced, eliminated, burned, and run over them, you try to explain to *A* that no, those were not a lover, job, house, and dog; they were *your* lover, job, house, and dog. *A* affects contrition but really has no idea what you're talking about.

❖

A hypothesizes and speculates, enjoys abstractions, prefers conjecture to conclusion. Nothing perplexes *A* more than hearing someone say, "We've got to find an answer!" "Find one?" thinks *A*. "There are billions of them all around you!"

❖

A offers up its noun for our consideration, evaluation, and possible adoption or acquisition. *A*'s an auctioneer.

❖

In T. S. Eliot's poem "The Love Song of J. Alfred Prufrock," the intensely conflicted title character asks himself a lot of questions, among them "Do I dare / Disturb the universe?" and "Do I dare to eat a peach?"

It seems like disturbing the universe should be a far more daring and difficult challenge than eating a peach. But in fact the first question is easier to answer than the second, because it permits only two possible answers, yes or no. The problem of

10

the peach, because it is burdened with the indefinite article, is more complicated. Before he could begin to solve it, Prufrock would first have to feel confident he'd chosen—from amongst all the peaches which have existed, presently exist, and will or might exist in the future—the correct peach to dare to eat. From the correct branch, tree, orchard, and planet, on the correct day at the correct hour by the correct hand, and so forth.

We shouldn't be surprised if in the end Prufrock finds it easier to disturb the universe than to eat a peach. The universe has been chosen for him. The universe is a sitting duck. But he'll never have the nerve to eat a peach.

❖

Brisk and efficient, *A* arrives early, in advance of its master, the complacent noun, to throw open a window, light a lamp, prepare the throne where the noun will settle its bulk. *A* exists to serve. *A*'s meaningless without its master. But they both know who really runs the household.

❖

And how does *A*'s noun regard its article? As a threat. *A* makes its noun feel dispensable and vulnerable. If a sweater itches, you can put on another. The discarded sweater is left to itch itself on the closet floor.

❖

Fantasies can't survive without the indefinite article, and can't survive the definite. W. B. Yeats, in his poem "The Lake Isle of Innisfree," begins dreaming of leaving the city for an idyllic rural retreat, where he'll build "a small cabin" and keep "a hive for the honeybee." But as soon as he starts trying to pin his whimsy down and muscle it into existence by using the definite article, determining to "live alone in the bee-loud glade," where evening's "full of the linnet's wings," the bubble bursts, and he finds himself right back where he started, standing "on the roadway, or on the pavements gray."

To keep a fantasy alive, be sure it remains *A* fantasy.

❖

A advocated early to put a man on a moon, supported a compromise of putting a man on the moon, and finally withdrew in disgust when the first astronaut climbed down the ladder to take the first steps in the dust.

I mean this very literally.

As we all know, Neil Armstrong, the astronaut in question, surveyed the moon's surface and said, "That's one small step for man, one giant leap for mankind." A sentence which, unfortunately, makes no sense. Armstrong later claimed he actually said, "That's one small step for a man, one giant leap for mankind," which *would* make sense (and also convey a disarming, if not quite believable, sense of humility), but everyone assumed he was just trying to cover up his mistake.

In 2006, an Australian computer programmer named Peter Shann Ford performed a sophisticated digital analysis of the original recording of Armstrong's lunar one-liner and concluded Armstrong had in fact used an *A* as he claimed, but had voiced the word for only thirty-five milliseconds, a duration detectable by computer software but ten times too fast to be audible to his listeners.

I'm sure no one wants Armstrong to suffer over this any more than he has, and I hope Ford's research brings him some peace in his old age. Still, the truth is clear. It was a moment of intense historical specificity, absolutely infested with instances of the definite article, and *A* wanted nothing to do with it.

❖

At night, *A* lies out in a meadow, contentedly counting a star, a star, a star. . . .

❖

A and *one* can sometimes stand in for each other. They're fraternal but not identical twins. Whether a genie allows you a wish or one wish, you know you've got one coming. But where the latter suggests you'd better not count on any more, the former teases you with the possibility.

One opens the door and then shuts it tight: the movie ticket says, "ADMIT ONE." *A* opens the door, admits one, and then leaves the door ajar in case your friends want to sneak in later.

If you're pretty sure you're going to have more than one, you say, "Sure, I'll have a drink." If you think you might mean to have only one: "I'll have *a* drink." If you're certain you mean to have only one: "I'll have one drink." If you're certain, serious, slightly annoyed, don't really want even one, and are already anticipating protest from your good-for-nothing friends: "I'll have *one* drink."

❖

A suspends and holds in abeyance. *A* loses track of time. A moment, a year, an appointment, a deadline. There will always be another.

❖

Try, in conversation, saying, "You know, the other day, a . . . ," and then just keep drawing out the *A*'s sound, like an oboe setting the pitch for an orchestra. This will drive your companion insane with impatience. Yes, yes, a *what?* A hand grenade? A heart attack? A big fat raise? A cricket in the kitchen?

Obviously, the suspense you're generating in your companion is primarily cognitive. Your *A* has opened a door in her mind, and she is waiting to see what will walk in. But am I just imagining it, or does *A*'s sound spoken aloud also seem to carry a certain purely musical suspense, like the sound of a minor chord left unresolved?

❖

Teams of two *A*s will sometimes work together to broker an agreement of equivalence, either numerical or metaphorical, between two nouns. One *A* ushers in the party of the first part; another (sometimes in the guise of *per*) introduces the party of the second part and closes the deal. These arrangements often result in proverbs:

An apple a day keeps the doctor away.

A night with Venus and a life with mercury.

A friend in need is a friend indeed.

A little learning is a dangerous thing.

This kind of work, with its emphasis on utility and communal values, appears to run contrary to *A*'s generally iconoclastic, dreamy, and solitary personality. Perhaps *A* considers it charity work. Or slumming.

❖

A noiseless, patient spider,
I mark'd, where, on a little promontory, it stood, isolated;

Mark'd how, to explore the vacant, vast surrounding,
It launch'd forth filament, filament, filament, out of itself;
Ever unreeling them—ever tirelessly speeding them.

And you, O my Soul, where you stand,
Surrounded, surrounded, in measureless oceans of peace,
Ceaselessly musing, venturing, throwing,—seeking the
     spheres, to connect them;
Till the bridge you will need, be form'd—till the ductile
     anchor hold;
Till the gossamer thread you fling, catch somewhere, O my
     Soul.

Walt Whitman's short poem "A Noiseless Patient Spider" begins with one of my favorite *A*'s in literature. Like its noun, this *A* seems packed with possibility and potential, but at the same time—also like its noun—it's pitiable, because it's racked with uncertainty about its place in the world. Like a spider's, *A*'s attachments are always temporary and insubstantial. Whenever *A* fixes itself to a noun, it knows one of two things will shortly happen, both of them bad news for *A*. Either the noun will not be mentioned again, or it will be, but this time preceded by the definite article *the*. In either case, *A* is out of a job, and must find a new noun to attach itself to.

(*A*'s addiction to the new is pathological. Or maybe it's better to say that its dependence on the new is pathetic.)

Whitman, as we might expect, admires the spider's ceaseless explorations. But he worries about the spider, too, fearing that with nothing and nowhere to call its own, to attach permanently and securely, it might die of disconnection. By the poem's end, Whitman has found a way for both the spider and his soul to anchor themselves, at least provisionally. In order to secure those connections, he has to deploy the definite article four times in the poem's last three lines. The destabilizing *A* is banished. But perhaps not saddened. Afoot and light-hearted, it takes to an open road, healthy and free, a world before it.

❖

A's a languorous and inventive but ultimately frustrating lover, because it lacks any understanding of completion.

❖

A is the fifth most commonly used word in the English language, according to the British National Corpus, a 100-million-word collection of samples of written and spoken English. Given *A*'s ubiquity, it's strange to contemplate the possibility that it may be entirely unnecessary. After all, it barely exists. When I listen to myself say aloud, "I need a pair of shoes," the *A* is almost unvoiced, a nearly indiscernible "uh" created by a quick clench in the throat.

I devise an experiment. I enter a shoe store and say distinctly to the clerk, "I need pair of shoes." She understands me perfectly. I go around like this all day, breaking in my new shoes and giving *A* a break. "Did you have good weekend?" "Cup of coffee, please." "Do you have four quarters for dollar?" "Should we go grab bite to eat and then catch movie?"

I get a few funny looks, but no one fails to understand me.

No one seems to miss *A* at all.

❖

A is fundamentally public and populist. *A* has nothing to hide, which is lucky, because it couldn't hide anything if it wanted to. It can be attached to anything, but it owns nothing; its greatest power is its ability to grant universal access to its noun.

Martin Luther King, Jr., told the crowd, "I have a dream." "I have" may have suggested personal possession, but the *A* made abundantly clear to everyone that a dream is ours to share.

❖

I call my wife at work and ask her to pick up *A* at the supermarket on her way home.

"A what?"

"We need *A* for dinner."

"A *what*?"

"Actually, you should probably also get *A* or two."

"Two *WHAT*?"

"No, on second thought, just *A* will be fine."

A pause. My wife is very smart. And more patient with me than I deserve.

"OK, see you soon."

She brought home *A* and I cooked it with *A* and *A*. Everything was delicious.

AMMAVIDE | Meena Alexander

It was only two years ago that I learned the Malayalam word *ammavide*—mother house, ancestral house, literally "mother's house." How can this be? I have been speaking the language since earliest childhood, ever since I could speak, and how is it that I never knew this word? But perhaps I knew it and have forgotten that I knew. Can this be? Imagine not having the word for what one writes about, over and over, in poems and prose. The house of my childhood, a Kerala house with red-tiled roof, and sandy courtyard where the mulberry tree my grandmother planted once bloomed; a house with whitewashed walls and high teak ceilings; a long, cool front verandah and pillars and parapets. A house that stands where the monsoon storms break, a house floating in clouds. After the first house, I want to say, there is no other. *Avede, evida, vide evida, avide, vide avide.* I have written this string of words, transliterated from Malayalam, to try to evoke what pours through me—*There, where, where is the house, there, house is there.*

ARDOR | Laura Jacobs

I like saying it, how it slows you down. Those two syllables—
the first made of air and the second of earth—meet strangely.
Unlike the slippery word *love,* so overused and abused, *ardor*
implies precision, a commitment to meaning.

Ardor is related to *ardent,* which flies like an arrow—swift
in desire, pointed—and means "burning." There is an ache
in *ardent,* as if the intensity is too strong and runs the risk of
disappointment. In *ardor* there is an arc. *Ardor* is arboreal:
Arcadia, Arden, Eden. It is green and growing, with as much
cooling shade in its realm as sun.

Ardor is Arthurian, a romance higher and larger than love,
mated to an idea or an ideal. It is perhaps more masculine than
feminine: pennants snapping in the breeze, buoyant with duty,
a moral dimension stitched to its breast. It is a word I admire
because it goes beyond narrow obsession: pleasures of the bed,
sheets that must be changed. *Ardor* gives more than it takes; it
is not about oneself, but about the subject that blossoms under
its arc of sky.

As (we like it) | Brenda Hillman

. . . so says Carol's email, as I ask her about *as*. *As* does a lot of work without being noticed—

As is an adverb, "antecedent" or "relative," a conjunction, a preposition—a word that can precede, connect, be swallowed, used twice in the same phrase. As bright as gold (adverb). It can be stuffed into other words with great frequency and make itself solidly known in a multitude of material existences.

"A worn-down form of *all-so*" says the *O.E.D.*, a phrase giving *as* (possessive noun) an etymology with a rather tragic cast (though perhaps all etymologies have a tragic cast) as (conjunction) it arrives from Old English. It sees itself as (preposition) a process poem.

"That not-as-clean-as-it-used-to-be oven was starting to skip certain temperatures."

I like the way *as* is so versatile, as is a poem or a person. Unlike many beloved nouns—*celadon*, for example, into which people peer, from which they peer away, trying to match the word to its locale or object—*as* is almost wispy. A vaporous maze that was always meant to connect.

Sight
But not so sweet
As we have seen
        —Jack Spicer, *Imaginary Elegies*

Also (a middle version of *as*), after reading an etymo-novella of the birth of *as* in the dictionary, I am amazed that "as bright as gold" began as a version of "so bright so gold." This *as* feels like a "tragic cast." We were always trying to get back to an original gold—or so thought the middle tribes, hammering away at bronze.

Etymology of *as*—as Yeats refers to the beard of God winding among the stars (curlicue@stars.com) in *A Vision*. David Lukas describes cirrus clouds and orthographic clouds ᴂᴇ̃ᴂ̃ as mountain writing, pointing over a ridge in the Sierra.

The boulders running by as cars
As cars running by as Art Blakey
        —Gabriel Gomez

Worn down, a progressive rubbing away as (conjunction) a word shifts, and then accretes to itself a new strength, a different strength, a pleasant or an unpleasant strength—

A simile is characterized by *like* or *as*, said Mrs. Lewis in seventh grade. But really, it turned out, more "like."

As my father's family ate squirrels in Mississippi during the Depression. "Head and all," he says.

Later we visit the same county, noticing the short dialect sentences almost as topiary next to the Sea Breeze RV Park.

"Ideas. As they find themselves." (Barbara Guest, *Rocks on a Platter*) (That seems pure conjunctive use of it—except it's a fragment. The use of *as* as adverb seems to be able to have *such* in front of it—the conjunctive use does not?)

Loving the way tiny areas of time sleep within letters of

the word or words . . . one day in the library stacks, before the library became so sadly neglected, my eye fell on *As I Lay Dying* on the back of a spine. In the crown, the loft below the high roof of the *A* . . . at the turn of the twenty-first century, I tried to write about this *as* enchantment with library dust.

Each word an utterance, a sound recalled in units of meaning. Who wouldn't want to be such a word as *as* when one grows up? *As*—so intense and helpful even if barely noticed!

For Carol Snow, Kristin Hanson, and Lyn Hejinian

BAFFLE | Albert Mobilio

Let me entertain you with some sleight of hand. Pick a card and slip it back in the deck. Put the deck in your back pocket and then, excuse me, as I shove you, so sorry, into this convenient and picturesque well. If you don't drown sputtering for air in its dank confines and you manage to climb out, your hands torn raw on the stone wall, you will find in the bucket dangling from the windlass just that card you selected so long ago before your near-death encounter. Would you not say my legerdemain *baffles* you? And thus confused, as stock expectations regarding a magic trick compete vigorously in your mind with what can only be termed a violent assault, do you find your ideation tangled, perhaps stickily so—as if, in sorting this out, you are struggling, tar-baby-like, with taffy? Whatever opinion you may pull free is bound to be arbitrary, your process of decision a bit of, say, a raffle. A raffle amid taffy, a mixed metaphor that baffles. Are you feeling the chilled bath now? If not, I'm only too happy to help you. Keats said axioms are not axioms till they are proved upon the pulse. Perhaps the same holds true for each and every word. We must feel the syllables against our skin. So I'll have that wallet of yours, thank you very much. Is this your driver's license? Were you ill the day this photo was taken? With those circles under your eyes, well, you looked careworn, and even generously assessed, somewhat desperate, bearing the aspect of a wanted man. Wrongly accused, no doubt. Bafflement at an unjust accusation; someone whose fate is about to be raffled off. You look troubled today, too, as well you might. Jaw slightly slack, mouth moving to the inaudible tune of surprise as you watch me cut your license into shreds, a dozen or more flakes of laminated paper fluttering to the ground. Bedeviled you surely are. But let me soothe you with the straight story, a clue made emphatic by whispering it close while grazing this lovely pair of needle-nosed pliers along the edge of your ear: Would you mind getting down on your knees and picking up every scrap to reassemble that card exactly as it was? Don't miss a piece! It's a jigsaw dilemma, isn't it? Not the same kind of puzzle as that 500-piece reconstruction of Yosemite Falls you did one summer at camp (almost every damn piece was granite-gray!). That was merely something you did. This puzzle is actually what you are— at this precise moment. It's what you're feeling: disconcerted, the flow of your thought impeded. Behind some battlement. Yes, you're impeded there on the sidewalk, shivering, uncertain, your glasses sliding down your nose as you pinch at the flecks of your card. What does he want, you surely must be thinking. When will he stop, you're asking yourself. So many questions your eyes eloquently pose even as they squint and dart over the pavement. And these questions don't go unnoticed. I'm impeded, too. Deflected for a moment, my rolling stride of sentences tripped up and suddenly stuck. I am looking down at you—and just *where* are you going to be—and my thoughts dash back and forth like children at recess, like bees from the hive

one child has struck. My thinking's doubly-mixed words fly off
aimed at this and that. Oh, yes, I'm deeply baffled, too. Baffled
but somehow waking. And daylight is the puzzle next.

BITCHIN' | Star Black

The word, burned into my brain as a preteen by the aimless sun on the beaches of California and Hawaii during the proto-popular surfing days of the late fifties and early sixties, is *bitchin'*, which means, rather than "bitch" or "bitchy," cool, suave, right on, awesome. It faded from my vocabulary when I moved East to attend college, and I rarely hear it today, aside from occasional visits to Napoopoo Bay on the Kona coast of the Big Island where Captain Cook was killed by the Hawaiians in the late eighteenth century. But it is there, ready, like surfing, for a cult revival.

BLOG | Katherine DeLorenzo

[Not too long ago, a much younger woman with whom I was chatting suggested casually that I might want to check out her blog. That is how she said it: "Would you like to check out my blog sometime?" Never mind that I had no idea what a blog was, or what exactly checking out this particular blog entailed. Wise people, as Kenko has stated, know how to keep their mouths shut. The context was some reference to essay writing, but I was at a loss to determine the exact connection. Was I being propositioned in some subtle manner that had escaped my notice? Was it a new brand of shoe, like Flucvog? A museum-shop Henry Moore reproduction, made from what had been a bloggy lump of self-hardening clay?]

A blog is a public online commentary uploaded to a portal or an Internet page, usually consisting of either a thematic enterprise involving one's week, day, or evening, or simply random thoughts strung together. *To blog* means to be literally publishing "real time" in cyberspace. Generally, the given etymology is *weblog*, but this is not quite as accurate as is commonly believed. Server administrators in the late 1990s, dealing with an enormous backlog of data, discovered their bandwidth overburdened with hefty chunks of hypertext and personal essays, resulting in *backlog*, which became known as *blog*, as in: "A blog crashed my server last night." Like *log*, it is a journal; a log is also a bulky piece of unshaped lumber and is very much, indeed, like a blog. It has been suggested that *blog* is really an amalgam of *log*, *blind*, *backlog*, and *slog*. *To blog* is to totter blindly through a thick sludge of late-night blogging, until some hitherto obscure understanding is reached and sleep can be resumed. A new *blogsticker* on one site proclaims this boldly with "Whereas I was once blind, now I blog."

A website interface named Blogger has been developed to handle the technical aspects of blogging, so that one may now blog with confidence. Other offspring of the verb *to blog* have proven less widespread, such as the use of *blogificate*, *textblogging*, and *blogganing*, which suggests a swift, luge-like descent down a slippery semantic slope. Blogs are often described as "meta-commentary" within a blog "meta-community" of blog-rings. This is something of a misnomer, although the prefix has been frequently enough applied to make this origin clear, such as "What's the meta with you? You knew your mother was going to read your blog!" Gary Turner has referred to blogs as *poem frites*: "Small chips of poetry, the fast-food equivalent [of poetry], instant wisdom, deep-fried. . . ." And on occasion, indigestible. There are different kinds of blogs: topic-oriented blogs, multi-user blogs, and blogs that simply exist for no other purpose than to revel in their unique blogness. "The vanity page is dead; long live the Blog!" pronounced John Dvorak (*PC Magazine*, February 5, 2002). Spinoffs of the term *blog* are the Bloggie Awards, Wil Wheaton blogs, RuPaul blogs. To blog is human; to crossblog, divine.

Blog is also linked to the well-known use of *blurb*, as in *blurb-log*. "Just a note that Ray has a new e-poetry collection out.

Buy it and help keep this blog-ring running. Every donation counts. Yes, we take PayPal!" Mac bloggers use iBlogs. There are sexblogs, including a "Best of the Sexblogs" compendium.

On a final note, here is Jeneane Sessum of allied.blogspot. com, who posted this at 9:54 AM, December 27, 2001: "[C]onsider that blogging is writing. And consider today that you are dying as you blog."

CAREEN | Karen Stolz

If you tell people you like the word *careen*, they inevitably say, "Oh, like a car careens off the road?" But *careen* can do so much more.

> Aunt Sheree tossed the bag of cranberries onto the counter. Dozens of glittery burgundy orbs careened over the surface and bounced onto the floor. "Hey, who opened these?" Aunt Sheree shouted, her cat-eye specs lowered accusingly.

Cranberries careen. The word *careen* has a pleasant sound, features a bit of onomatopoeia. The *ca* swoops into the *reen*. To careen is to veer wildly. Sure, out-of-control cars do it. Drunks do it. But can't fools in love careen into each other's arms? Can't toddlers careen into grandma's flannel pajamaed legs? Can't a cat careen into her Whisker City toy? They can and they do. There can be a sort of exuberance to the word.

Let me confess right now: One reason I may like the word *careen* is that my name is Karen. So, *careen* is like a very cranked-up, jet-setty version of my name. Growing up with a vanilla name like Karen, you wish for some heady variations.

When you look up *careen* in the dictionary, you find words like *sway, lurch,* the phrase *keel over. Sway* can have a fetching connotation: hot, swaying bodies, for instance. *Lurch,* no. *Keel over* is usually for boats. But maybe, sometimes, we careen because we are knocked asunder (*asunder,* a swell word, too), just plain swept away.

Before I fell on ice concealed craftily under snow, I careened around a bit first. That's not a pleasant careening. But before I fell for guys (in my tender youth), there was a careening too, and the out-of-controlness felt at least partly good.

It's time we let verbs do more of the descriptive heavy lifting in writing. So, let's hear it for *careen,* a word that has been unfairly relegated to detailing vehicular mayhem. Because, sometimes, being in control and moving straight forward is not exciting. Sometimes, to careen is to let go, to be enraptured, to soar.

COLANDER | Lee Martin

One summer morning, the telephone rang in my grandmother's house, and, because she was busy washing dishes at the sink, I ran to answer it. She kept the new dial phone on a library table by her bedroom window, a bedroom off the kitchen in the modest frame house where I'd spent the night. It was 1962, and I was seven years old. Progress had come to our sleepy, backwoods part of southern Illinois in the form of telephones you dialed instead of cranked, and seven-digit numbers instead of a series of long rings and shorts. My grandmother had all this before my parents did in our farmhouse just two miles east on the County Line Road.

My grandmother's phone was on a party line, and I loved to sneak into the bedroom when she was occupied with her soap opera—she was faithful to *As the World Turns*—and pick up the receiver and eavesdrop on other people's conversations. "Well, I swan," I heard a woman say one day, and I thought how marvelous it sounded when she said it, her voice nearly breathless with disbelief. "I swan." More splendid than it sounded when my grandmother said it. More wonderful because it came to me over that phone line, a voice without a body, just the pure sound of it.

When the phone rang on that summer morning and I answered it, a woman's voice on the other end of the line said to me, "Lee, tell Grandma to bring her calendar."

It was my Aunt Anna, my mother's sister, and I said, all right, I would. I'd tell Grandma that instant. *A calendar,* I may very well have thought to myself. *I swan.*

I ran into the kitchen, and I tugged on my grandmother's apron. "Aunt Anna's on the phone," I said, "and she wants you to bring your calendar. Hurry. Quick."

Grandma whisked a calendar from the nail where it hung next to the crank phone she no longer used. She hurried into the bedroom, where I'd left the receiver lying on the library table. She picked up the receiver and held it to her ear. She said, "Anna. I've got the calendar. What's wrong?"

But there was no answer on the other end of the line, and my grandmother looked at me with suspicion in her narrowed eyes, her bunched-up brow. She laid the receiver into its cradle. How I loved that sleek, black phone with its dial that whirred along so merrily when I put a finger into one of its notches and spun it. "Lee," my grandmother said, "it's not nice to story."

She thought I was fibbing, but I wasn't. Aunt Anna was on the phone. She said, "Tell Grandma to bring her calendar." Now suddenly she wasn't there. Just silence, and I said to my grandmother, "Just ask her when she comes to get us."

Aunt Anna was coming in her car, and she and I and my grandmother were going to my parents' farmhouse where my mother was canning tomato juice.

"Not me," Aunt Anna said when she arrived and my grandmother asked her whether she'd called. Once again, I was suspect.

"Little boys who tell stories grow long noses," my grandmother said, and I kept quiet, not knowing what to say in my defense.

❖

For the most part, I was a shy boy, an only child, but somehow I picked up a knack for performance. Given the right circumstances, I could be a ham. My father was a storyteller, animated and full of pizzazz. My mother, like me, was timid. I remember how she sang hymns in church, her voice so soft, only I, sitting next to her, could hear it.

What a surprise, and I hope a delight, it must have been when she discovered that her son, despite his shyness, enjoyed putting on a show—loved, in fact, the music words could make.

I could do voices, and most of those voices came from television, to which I was hopelessly addicted: Walter Cronkite's, "And that's the way it is"; Jackie Gleason's, "And away we go"; Red Skelton's, "Good night, and may God bless." I could do Fred Flintstone ("Yabba Dabba Do"), Popeye ("I yam what I yam"), Elmer Fudd ("Ooh, that wascally wabbit"). Sometimes I'd come to the supper table after watching a western on TV where a hardened cowboy had the fortune of a home-cooked meal, and, when I was finished eating, I'd say to my mother, "Much obliged for the vittles, ma'am." Other times, I'd burst out with my best Jimmy Cagney, "You'll never take me alive, coppers." Or I'd throw my arms around our collie's neck and wring the sap out of a line from that week's episode of *Lassie*: "Good girl, Lassie. Oh, Lassie. You've come home."

❖

My mother must have wondered who the heck I was, this boy who otherwise would cling to her skirts in the presence of strangers and hope against hope that no one noticed him, or worse yet, spoke to him, or god forbid asked him a question that required an answer. I was that boy a good deal of the time. A mommy's boy. Even now, it slices me to say the words, to know the truth of them. But there they are. I was the boy who, for a few months during second grade, worked himself into such a dither that it was easy to feign illness—all for the sake of staying home, close to my mother. My parents took me to the doctor, a gruff man who smoked cigars. He prescribed medication for my condition, a teaspoon of clear liquid each morning. In later years, I figured out it was sugar water. He suspected what ailed me was all in my head.

❖

It was in my heart, too, this feeling of dread. Really, that's what it was. A fear that sometime while I was at school, my mother and father would pack up and leave. In addition to being a farmer, my father was a CIA operative, dispatched in the middle of the night, with a sudden call, to places I could only imagine: Moscow, or Buenos Aires, or East Berlin. His farming was his cover; nothing about our lives was real. Only I didn't know that then. I just knew that sometimes I came home, and my father was gone. He stayed gone for days on end, and, when I asked my mother where he was, she simply said, "Traveling."

No, that's a lie. A transparent one at that. You knew it as soon as you read it, didn't you? You see what I mean about who I am? A shifter of words, an actor, a liar. I had friends at school and friends on the farms near to ours, but like all only children, I spent the bulk of my childhood entertaining myself. I made up stories. I never stopped. Yet here's the truth. My father was a farmer. He lost both of his hands in a cornpicker when I was a year old. He wore "hooks." He could be an angry man. I was a boy, watching for the signs that he was about to explode, about to take off his belt, or reach for a yardstick, and whip me. When his rage filled our home, I shrieked and howled, and that was me, the most genuine me I could be, the one wailing—all lungs and throat and nerves and skin.

❖

But there was joy, too. In the midst of my father's terror, we found ways to love each other. My family was knotty and difficult to define. Any attempt requires sifting through the layers of our contradictions. I was the shy boy who could cozy up to the spotlight. My father could be the fun-loving rake one moment, dark and brooding the next. And my timid mother, who one night said she was fed up with the both of us and she was going, just going. She didn't know where, and I think she might have if I hadn't stopped her. If I hadn't thrown my arms around her legs and begged her to stay. No performance that, and even if it had been it would have been a melodrama at best, a real scenery-chomper. "Don't go. Please. I'll be good. Don't go." That's what I said, and I meant every word, as honestly and as urgently as I've ever meant anything my whole life.

❖

Sitting here now, I try to recall my mother's voice, and I can almost manage it, but not quite. You'd think we'd remember forever the way our parents spoke, but it's not really the truth, is it? Their voices, once they're dead, become a stir of air, a tingle on the skin, a thrumming in our chests, a murmur heard, fuzzy with static, on a phone line—you know the sort I mean, that voice from another line bleeding over into the background of your own conversation; you swear you can almost make out what it says.

36

When I was small, my mother read to me at bedtime. It's the rhythm of her voice I can recall better than the voice itself, a cadence temperate and soothing, a tempo steady with comfort and care, a pace pulsing with what she believed all her life—what she'd learned from giving herself over to faith—the conviction that on the other side a peace waited for us all. Her name was Beulah, an old-fashioned name these days, but one that fit her. Beulah, the promised land in John Bunyan's *Pilgrim's Progress*. Beulah, the heavenly Zion. I could hear her name sung at our little country church: "O Beulah Land, Sweet Beulah Land." When I try to recall her voice now, I think of that church and drowsy summer Sundays when the windows were open and the breeze came in enough to ruffle the tissue-thin pages of New Testaments. That whisper. That was my mother.

But then there was that night she threatened to leave, and that was another sound of her voice, ugly with misery and grief, as when years later she looked down at my father in his casket and said, in a voice quaking and raw, "I don't even have a picture of him." She had that voice, too, and that's the one it hurts me most to recall because if anyone deserved to avoid the bang and truck too common to our family, it was her.

❖

I have to believe, though, she was happy to have us. Once upon a time, she was an old-maid schoolteacher at forty-one, still living with her parents, surely imagining that she'd already made her life. She'd go on teaching school, seeing to other women's children. She'd work in my grandparents' general store evenings and Saturdays, surrounded by people like my father, not knowing that one evening he'd stay after hours on the pretense of helping her close up the store. He was thirty-eight, a bachelor farmer taking care of his ailing mother. I wonder what he said to my mother that night at the store. Did he make a joke, cut her a shy grin? Did he look down at his shoes, stuff his hands in his pockets? Or did he look her straight in the eye, explain to her that he was a man of a certain age, and she was a woman of like years, and there they were, neither one of them with prospects and wouldn't it make sense if they tried things out for a while just to see if maybe they might be able to get on?

Imagine my mother that night on her short walk across the road to the modest frame house where she lived with my grandparents, taking her time as she moved through the twilight. I don't know whether this night fell in spring. I don't know whether there was light at all, but I prefer to think there was what folks used to call the *gloaming*, that half-light fading fast. I like to imagine the melancholy call of rain birds, a breeze moving through the branches of the oak trees, the lush white pom-pom blossoms of a snowball bush, and my mother memorizing all this so she could recall it time and time again before she finally said, "I'm in love with Roy Martin."

❖

I wish I could keep her there on that night and save her from what's to come, that day in early November 1956, when she gets the call about my father's accident, and the surgeon has to amputate, when she knows that she and my father are moving into a way of living they never could have seen coming. Twenty-six more years to navigate, my mother doing for my father the things he can no longer do himself: shaving, bathing. When he finishes with the toilet, he whistles for her. A soft, low whistle from behind a closed door. An embarrassed, "I need you," and that's another sound I remember from my childhood.

"Beulah, peel me a grape!" Mae West orders her character's maid in the 1933 movie *I'm No Angel.*

To type the line now saddens me because I relied on my mother to keep me happy just as my father relied on her for his needs. We often treated her as if she were our servant. I was simply lazy. It was easier to ask her to bring me a soft drink while I was watching television than to get up and go into the kitchen and fetch it myself. When my father died, and my mother found herself alone in their house, she told me it was the first time all her life that she had no one to take care of. "I don't know what to do with myself," she said.

❖

She used to tell me it wasn't up to us to question the circumstances of our lives. It was our job, instead, to live them as best we could, to trust that God had a plan for each of us, to know that something that looked like a curse could just as easily be a blessing. I have to admit I don't have the same degree of conviction as she did. I lean more toward my father's skepticism. He knew that sometimes the world has plans for us that ask too much. How could he have possibly felt any differently after that day in the cornfield? He was a man about to shut down his tractor and gather up his wife and son and go to his sister's and brother-in-law's house for supper. Then he tried to clear the picker's clogged shucking box; his hands got caught between its rollers, and suddenly he was a different man. It could happen that quickly. That's what my father learned, the way a life could divide into before and after.

❖

My mother was an old-maid schoolteacher, and then she was a wife. She was a wife for four years, and then she was a mother. She was a mother a little over a year. Then my father's accident made her his caretaker. Through it all, she loved God. All signs point toward this: She prayed to him each night, kneeling as she must have done since she was a little girl, and put her fingers to her lips. In the silence, something took place in her spirit that allowed her to keep moving forward, to sift through the facts of her life, to preserve the things that were good and right—I like to think I was one of them, one of the blessings that saved her.

❖

In the garden she kept each summer, she grew all sorts of vegetables: corn, beets, carrots, tomatoes, green beans, cauliflower, broccoli, peas, peppers, squash. Whatever she could put by for the winter, she did—cold-packed, pressure-canned, frozen—even after she lived alone. A young woman during the Great Depression, she'd learned there was always a day coming she couldn't predict, a day of want, perhaps, and it was always good to put a little something by just in case you needed it later.

Then her body betrayed her. She suffered from hypertension and eventually started having small strokes, Transient Ischemic Attacks that began with a tingle in her lip and moved down her left side, leaving her dizzy and listing. Eventually she suffered from dementia and spent the last few months of her life in a nursing home, aphasic, her speech a series of syllables and sounds, none of them cohering. I sat beside her and patted her hand. I told her I loved her, but I'm not sure she heard or understood.

After she moved to the nursing home, I readied her house for sale. I sorted through her belongings, saving for last the jars and jars of food she'd canned. As I handled those cool Mason jars and felt their weight, I recalled summer days, my mother's kitchen hot with tomatoes or corn or beans cooking on the stove, and canning jars sterilized with boiling water. My mother in her apron and hairnet, beads of sweat dripping from her nose, her cat-eye glasses steaming over when she leaned in to fill those jars with whatever she was intent on preserving. I can still hear the steam rising in the pressure canner, the release valve dancing and jiggling. What did I know, then, of the noise our living makes? The sounds that mark our give and take, the ones we sort and press and try to preserve?

❖

I remember this—a moment frozen in an eternal present:

On the day I tell my grandmother to bring her calendar and she later suspects me of telling a lie, we walk into our farmhouse, and my mother says, "Oh, good, you brought it."

My grandmother is holding her food mill, that kitchen tool used for grinding and pureeing. A deep metal pan with perforations in the bottom. A broad blade in its center at the end of a hand crank. After the tomatoes cook, my mother will press them through the food mill, turning the crank so the blade can cull out skins and seeds, and allow the juice to pass through the perforations, back into the cooking pot so she can boil it again before she pours it into the Mason jars. Part sieve, part mill; my mother calls it a colander, and I understand now she was the one on the phone.

As the years go on, she'll take great joy in telling the story of the day I thought she said *calendar,* but that day in our farmhouse, even though she's laughing because I confused her voice for my aunt's, the laughter finally fades away, and when it does I feel peculiar. It's something about the way my mother looks at me, disappointed, and I don't know what to call this thing I feel, so I seal it up inside me, where it waits to be turned and strained: this shame, this longing.

41

"Didn't you know?" she says, just a hint of hurt in her eyes. I wish I could tell her now, yes, I knew. I always knew. "Mercy," she says. "Didn't you know it was me?"

CORN | Katherine Karlin

Whatever happened to corn?

Not the grain. That's still very much with us, in our fuel and in everything we eat. By *corn* I mean the items in our culture that have passed into obsolescence, irrelevance, and bad taste. Corn is sentimental, kitschy, and unsophisticated. Corn is uncool.

When I was a girl, my ears were finely tuned to detect and reject corn. It was the sound of my parents' generation, qualitatively different from my own. Andy Williams was corny, as were Steve and Eydie, and Frank Sinatra. Maybe we were wrong about Sinatra, but we came by our mistake honestly; it takes the authentic experience of adult ennui to appreciate the malaise of "The Wee Small Hours of the Morning." But the Sinatra that found its way to the radio waves of my childhood—the bombast of "My Way" or the insincere romanticism of "Strangers in the Night"—*that* was pure corn.

Corn marks the break between one generation and the next. We needed only hear the opening strains of a song to know if it was corny or cool. Syrupy strings, bossa nova rhythms, a Mexican trumpet: corn. Dissonance, throbbing, and shouting were cool.

43

Corny songs were about cheating; cool songs described sexual urgency.

Corn wasn't only about pop music, either, although nothing quite defines a generation like its preference in pop music. Corn infiltrated every aspect of the culture. Soapy movies, in which fallen women suffered exquisitely, were corny. Social realism was corny; Beckett was cool. The homespun scenes of Norman Rockwell were corny, and the harsh alienation of Diane Arbus was cool. Nellie Forbush, the unflappable heroine of the Rodgers and Hammerstein musical *South Pacific,* proclaimed her love for a wonderful guy with the disclaimer that she was "corny as Kansas in August." Such unabashed emotion was corny. So were Rodgers and Hammerstein.

It wasn't a question of age so much as attitude. The Marx Brothers were old, but their anarchic irreverence was never corny. Sonny and Cher belonged to the Beatles generation, but they were never a part of the youth culture—they won their corn credentials when they were offered up as the conservative TV replacement to the very cool Smothers Brothers. Any attempt to appropriate coolness was automatically corny: take a look a *Rowan & Martin's Laugh-In* or Sinatra singing "Something."

In her slang lexicon *Dewdroppers, Waldos, and Slackers,* Rosemarie Ostler tells us that corn appeared in the 1930s among jitterbuggers. *Corny* or its derivatives, *on the cob* or *cornpone,* described the older set, who were countrified. For young, newly urban blacks, *corn* was a shorthand for differentiating themselves from their rural relations. It doesn't take much imagination to see why this distinction was necessary; coming into the cities, young blacks had uprooted themselves from the land, and with new, wage-earning jobs they enjoyed a new degree of independence, self-expression, and gender equity—all of which can be seen in the ecstatic steps of the jitterbug itself.

You don't hear much talk of corn anymore. In fact, saying

"corn" can date you like a mouthful of silver fillings. A possible explanation for the disappearance of *corn* is widespread cynicism that renders nearly any attempt at emotional traction—from political protest to linear narrative—as corny. The word has lost its currency.

But I think there's something else at work here, and that's the failure of the ascendant generation to define itself. Since the counterculture, which, like the jitterbuggers of the thirties, made a decisive break from all that preceded it, every five years a new term has struggled for posterity: yuppies, Gen-X, Gen-Y, the Echo Generation. None of these claimed an identity that had any legs. If a cohort has this much trouble defining itself, it can't possibly cast aspersions on its elders. And you see this amorphousness reflected in the pop culture. Bands like U2 that were around twenty years ago are still beloved. *The Godfather* remains a movie favorite. Young singers approximate the sound of Dusty Springfield or Al Green. When I was a kid, stories about a Glenn Miller concert would induce only eye-rolling. But tell a teenager today you spent a night sleeping in the mud to see the Grateful Dead and she won't think it's corny; she'll think it's awesome. Part of me feels a little smug about my enduring resistance to corn. But the curmudgeon in me screams, *Get your own damned icons.*

Add to this the notion that anything that hangs around long enough becomes cool by dint of mere survival. How else to explain the sudden enthusiasm for Neil Diamond? Burt Bacharach, the very soul of corn, is making records with Elvis Costello, than whom none is cooler. The recently-canceled television show *Boston Legal* costarred William Shatner and Candice Bergen; the dark prince of middle-brow American geekdom and the aloof goddess of the French New Wave shared a small screen, and even a kiss or two. That these two intractably parallel lines converged, albeit late in life, explodes the very concept of corn itself. Corn is not supposed to mix with cool, but wither in isolation.

Perhaps what really killed corn is the very postmodern, nonjudgmental blurring of high and low culture. When we look at cultural phenomena not in terms of their aesthetics, but in terms of what conditions made them possible, they all have value. Accordion music may grate the ear, but when you understand the polka in its context of the American immigrant experience, it is laden with significance. Embedded in this approach is an egalitarianism that extends not only to cultures but to generations, as well. Corn has disappeared not because of cynicism but a surfeit of sweetness.

CRASH | Dan Moyer

"Did you ever notice that the Cowardly Lion sounds a lot like Snagglepuss?"

This is what I wake up to. This is how the day greets *me*. With stupid questions about classic television.

"You awake yet, buddy? Eh?"

My friend kneels beside the bed and shakes me just hard enough to constitute an annoyance. My friend, that is, Slimer, who's named for his flabby midsection, is fully dressed. His hair is parted to one side. Jacket already buttoned. Shoes double-knotted. He sits there and shakes shakes shakes me, smiling this conniving little smirk.

I manage to grunt the word *no.*

"Come on, man. I got to get back for work." Slimer peeks down at his watch and says, "It's already one o'clock."

One o'clock, I tell myself. My day starts at one o'clock.

The freshness of morning has long since come and gone. The chirping birds have been silenced. That smell—the one of new leather and coffee and sunshine—has been outdone by a stronger stench, one of vomit and uncontrolled perspiration.

I no longer feel asleep yet cannot be awakened. It is an awkward stage. A limbo, if you will. A purgatory where my half-naked body floats endlessly through a dreamlike hallway of white. Wrapped in bed linens. And on this particular morning (or is it afternoon?), I dream up a vision of Slimer, who is still shaking me. It is only one o'clock.

"All right. I'm up. I'm up." With a tremendous effort I roll to the left, freeing myself from the blanket and an unknown pair of legs. Slimer stands up as I place my right foot, then my left, squarely on the floor. Rock back and forth a few times to gain a sense of balance in the world. Run my chapped fingers through my hair and ruffle it up a bit.

Slimer looks at me with a mindless gaze stapled to his face and asks, "Did you think about it? You know, about the whole Cowardly Lion and Snagglepuss thing?"

"No. No, I did not."

While I'm gathering the energy to attempt to stand, Slimer says, "Looks like YOU had a good time last night," and follows this with a point over my shoulder. Sprawled out across the rest of the bed is some blonde with thick curls and a dove tattooed on her left shoulder. Her name is Sandy. I think. Or along the lines of any "Andy"-sounding name. Other possibilities include, but are not limited to, Candy, Mandy, and Randi. She's naked except for a single sock which clings to a last few toes.

"I couldn't really tell you," I say, standing up. "Don't really remember." I'm wearing a pair of striped boxers. Zebra-striped, of course. I tell Slimer to relax for a minute while I get dressed. Hearing this news, which I suppose demeaned him, or frustrated him in some sense, Slimer heads back toward the living room. I watch as he plops down on the couch next to another sleeping body scrunched in the fetal position.

About a minute later (or perhaps it was two) I scrounge through a clutter of clothes and notebooks and wires, searching for car keys. The room, which resembles more of a war zone than an actual bedroom, is sullied with crumbs and other shreds of garbage. Proof of last night's food fight, which included, but was not limited to, Goldfish, pretzels, and gourmet peanuts. The scene is best described as chaotic. Cookies and chocolate are ground deep into carpet fibers. A light bulb lies shattered atop an overturned end table. Empty bags and wrappers, which are scattered here and there, seem like outgrown shells on a beach. I feel bad for whomever this room belongs to.

For reasons I cannot fully explain at this point in time, I give the girl a kiss on the forehead and whisper goodbye. She responds with an "uhhgh" and wipes drool from her mouth. I take it as a "Thank you for such a wonderful time last night" kind of thing.

"Finally . . . ," Slimer groans as I round the corner into the living room. "Jesus Christ, I want to get out of here. This place reeks." He pinches his nose like a child and jumps to his feet. "Let's go."

There are another six or seven people sleeping in various parts of the living room. There's the 110-lb. kid from the neighboring dorm curled up on the couch. Turns out he *is* my age. Not just some overachieving "I-was-coddled-too-much-during-infancy" kind of child genius.

To my right, underneath a set of broken blinds, are two girls spooning. At their feet, sleeping, I supposed, dangerously too close to their actual feet, is a guy wrapped in newspaper. On the other side of him is another guy. Wrapped in newspaper as well.

Across the room is my friend Squirrel. Utilizing a boot as a pillow, he's propped up against the wall. A *101 Dalmations* sleeping bag is thrown over his lower half. It was through Squirrel that Slimer and I had learned of this party. Squirrel is the friend of a friend of a friend who happened to sell the owner of the apartment some very fine marijuana once. As soon as word

49

spread about a party at 424C, Squirrel relayed the information, good friend that he is. In retrospect, I should have offered him one of the extra throw pillows from the bedroom.

I navigate my way through the living room—stepping over arms, legs, and even an exposed neck. I think to myself that the party's aftermath resembles a horrific massacre of some sort. St. Valentine's, perhaps. Dozens shot or stabbed and left to rot away with the rest of their surroundings. The sight is tragic. Even a tad revolting. Until I see the steady up-down, up-down of one girl's stomach, and I'm reminded that although they look dead, they are in fact very much alive.

Slimer opens his mouth and says, "You remember when the cops came last night?"

"No," I laugh. "Like I said before, I don't remember much. What time did they show up?" Slimer tells me probably somewhere between 1:30 and 3:45 AM, but assuredly no later than 4:15 AM. Noise complaint, of course, as it is almost every weekend at State. He says everyone thinks it was the nerds from down the hall, and concludes his rant with "I hate nerds" and an overly dramatic cracking of knuckles.

At the door, I do a final personal pat-down. Left and right pocket. Cell phone: check. Car keys: check. My back two pockets. Wallet: check. Condom: uncheck, but for worthwhile reasons. I visualize my body to be like a paper doll, and place articles of clothing on the appropriate sections. T-shirt: check. Sweater: check. Jeans, shoes, socks, belt: all check. Slimer's looking at me like the pissed-off child who's just learned Santa's not real.

"I am going to kill you," he mutters, spacing each word with a breath for added emphasis. "I swear to God."

I survey the living room a final time. The bodies, all dead yet very much alive, remain still. Silent. Some of the other victims include, but are not limited to: Jennifer, Ralph, Red Baseball Hat Guy, Gwen, Girl with Noticeably Too-Short Shorts,

and Crew Cut. All asleep. All victims of a night's night. Some
are splattered with dried vomit, while others remain unscathed.
There are guys with girlfriends snuggling with girls who are in
fact NOT their girlfriends. The few who drank too much and
embarrassed themselves—they will awaken with magic marker
scribbled across their faces. Or with debris from a fight, as is
apparent from the two guys with torn white shirts stained with
blood (both the opponent's and their own). The rest will simply
await the repercussions of their poor choices. This last group is
by far the most nerve-racked. Every guy waits for the "I'm late"
speech. Every girl, the "You should probably get tested" version.
Practically interchangeable, save for a few key phrases.

Last but certainly not least, there are myself and Slimer,
members of no particular clique at all. We await no message,
for that message is clear: these are the best times of our lives.

"You know what, Slimer?" He responds with a quick "What?"
even though I hadn't expected him to. "These are the best times
of our lives," I say. And he smiles and nods.

It is strange, I suppose, to be both the perp and the victim
of one's own circumstance. In our case, the college experience.
A time to let go, yet gain knowledge. A time to experiment with
drugs, but be careful. A time to black out and not care. Make
friends with strangers. Have sex without making love. And live
while slowly dying.

Taking the walk of shame down a set of slippery stairs, I
think about how this was all a result of a simple question last
night. A girl. A blonde. "Do you want to *crash*?" she had asked.

DÄMMERUNG | Susan Bernofsky

Dämmerung [dawn or dusk] has a Damm inside it, a dam to hold back the light. From here inside the house, the sky appears violet, it is undergoing a transformation. From darkness, the first sputtering of illumination appears, first in the form of a pale fluid suffusing everything above the horizon, then the liquid gels, sets, hardening and softening at the same time until all at once the light is everywhere, a successful invasion. This is the *Morgendämmerung* [dawn], the morning one, all rosy-fingered, the dimmer switch slowly cranked to full. A fine time to go strolling on the Ku'damm, as it is called here in Berlin, the Kurfürstendamm to be exact: the grand avenue named for the prince electors who once rode their horses upon a wooden path laid through the bog to get from their palace in town to a hunting lodge in the Grunewald Forest. They might have ridden at times through the *Abenddämmerung* [dusk]—since the dawn of evening is twilight—wishing to sup out in the forest amid crackling twigs and the cries of unseen beasts.

There are other sorts of *Dämmerung* as well, such as the *Götterdämmerung* [twilight of the gods], in which the gods crash and burn in German sagas or at the opera, and *Menschheitsdäm-merung* [twilight of mankind], the dawn of humankind, which is the title of a book of Expressionist poems.

The urban *Dämmerung* is all about smog: dawn and dusk alike pixilated with haze. *Dämmerung* can be mental, too, as we declare the arrival of an inkling as its dawning. Then the haze clears to reveal the outlines of a thought—one that, with any luck, we can hold on to for a while.

DARB | Erin McGraw

> **darb** *(darb)* *n.* 1920s slang for an excellent person or
> thing, e.g., "Vincent is the darb" the minute Vincent
> picks up the dinner check.

[As with much slang, the etymology is murky. The word could derive from the French *d'arbres,* "from the trees," as to indicate a high vantage point or, perhaps, superior fruit. This derivation does not seem likely.

[Much slang from the period reflected the popularity of jazz music. Pig Latin, for instance, could be likened to jazz in its application of traditional linguistic modalities. *Darb,* therefore, might have been an abbreviation for *darbay,* a reasonable Pig Latin transformation of *barbed,* which conceivably could have been adopted as an indicator of the ironic detachment that was a hallmark of the youth of that era. And every era.

[Barbed wire was invented in 1863.

[Alternatively, if Cockney-style rhyming slang had immigrated across the Atlantic with soldiers returning from the First World War, *darb* could have derived from *garb,* as in a well-dressed Vincent. Also, nothing rhymes with *darb* except *garb* and *barb*. This can't be right.

[*Derby*, as in a race, is pronounced "Darby" in Britain. Hence a derby winner might be pronounced a "darby winner," cheekily shortened to "darb" in a decade that was fond of shortness in many things, including skirts and hair. There is nothing whatever to support this notion, either. Who am I trying to fool?

[Slang—outlaw language, a huge scofflaw—erupts wherever it wants. Linguists admit that they can't figure out how words, before the Internet, before television, suddenly bloomed in the mouths of teenagers, ready-made to exclude those pitiful kids outside the mysterious circuitry and to mock adults. The *linguists* don't know. They're like blondes in blonde jokes— something else that just cropped up one day and took over like the ineradicable dandelions in my backyard, *dandelion* coming from "*dent de lyon*," or "lion's tooth," from the serrated shape of the leaf—shrugging their shoulders and shaking their bright heads and admitting, "I don't know." It's not good enough.

[When my husband's nephew was four years old, he went with his family to Florida. Walking along the beach, he grew more and more unnerved. "Where's the edge?" he wanted to know. Good question! Where's the edge? How are we supposed to know where we can build our houses and send our kids to school to verify their slang if we don't know where the edge is? Otherwise we could wake up to the cold water slopping over our bed. Somebody needs to tell us where the edge is. It isn't too much to ask.]

DASSN'T | Richard Terrill

"Dassn't scrap, dassn't scrap," my German grandpa intoned whenever my brother and I started poking each other's chest and belly in his sun-filled living room. At five years old, I wore the more serious expression of the two combatants, and I started most of the fights, egged on by a brother five years my senior who knew every match would end in his favor.

In the years just past mid century, my grandfather was already in his seventies, a thin wafer of a man with long ears and long nose—a man who, fifty years later, I have grown to resemble. He told stories—the same ones over and over, much to the chagrin of his only son-in-law, my father. "Grandpa is senile," we told each other, echoing my father's summary judgment, but now I'm not sure that was the problem. Rather, with repetition, the morals of Grandpa's tales were meant to crystallize: the story about the Indian who left the reservation and made a success, only to fall, through his profligate nature. He died with only a broken jackknife in his pocket. The boy who went swimming in a weedy bay, became tangled, and cried for help. His brother (or friend, or a passerby—someone) answered the call. Both drowned. Maybe that bay was near the lake in northern Wisconsin where our family had a summer cottage. Where we were going that next weekend.

With such repetition it's a wonder I can't remember more of these stories. Perhaps I too am getting senile. But I do remember well the singular unified message: *be careful.* Be careful swimming in that lake. Be careful with your money. *Dassn't do.* My grandfather perceived a dangerous world, the curse of my mother's childhood, she said, and perhaps her adult life as well, a forties and fifties housewife, shut in. But about the dangerous world, who's to say he wasn't right?

The Columbia Guide to Standard American English identifies *dassn't* as "a regional dialectal locution now archaic and reflective of our literary past." But most sources link the usage to a lack of education. My grandfather attended school only through the fifth grade (and German was the language of instruction). In the usual online sources and chats you can find *dassn't* ascribed to old rural Southern dialect—it shows up in *Tom Sawyer*, for instance. Gailr, the Grand Panjandrum, posts, "I originally invoked 'dassn't' in memory of my grandma R; her peeps were German immigrants. . . . She lived in the Midwestern 'Sam Hills' all her life. I don't know where she got it from, although I do know that higher education was not a priority for many of her generation."

No one disputes either the word's denotation or its origin. *Dassn't* is a contraction of *dare not.*

Teaching college in China in the 1980s, and fed up with the local Communist Party chief's iron rule over my fun-loving students, I once suggested to a group of young women they simply skip the required weekly Party meeting and go into town. Tell the Party Leader to jump in the lake.

Once I explained what I meant by that phrase, they replied

as if in one voice: "We dare not!" People dared not do many things in that part of the world at that time.

In the seventies, a Wisconsin governor chided the state legislature, run by the other party, with something to the effect of, "You dassn't cut state services in hard times." Or it may have been you dassn't cut taxes in hard times, I really can't remember. I do remember the usage merited a small piece in the newspaper that was picked up by the wire services. The governor did not return to office in the next election. You dassn't vote for a guy like that, the electorate must have concluded.

A few years ago over a beer at Christmas, my older brother and only living relative asked jokingly whether on my final exam the previous week I had made my college students conjugate the verb *dassn't. I dassn't, you dassn't, she dassn't.* We got a good laugh, but I think it was the family subtext that made it funny.

And just today at the supermarket an elderly man, stocky and walking with a cane, began yelling at the teller of the store's main branch bank. The bank could shove it, he yelled. The teller could shove it. He'd been coming here for fourteen years, but would never come again. Never.

I picked up a quart of milk and a pound of unsalted butter, returned to the checkout's long lines, a few days before Christmas, and the old man was yelling to the store manager now, even louder, standing near the automatic doors. Store customers, complacently, neatly in line, all watched him, facing the doors as they were. *Was he dangerous?* I could hear them think. Probably not. Too old.

Just last week, in the stress of final exam week at school, I yelled in a meeting with my colleagues. We were arguing and I thought I was right, still think I was, seven days hence. But in hindsight I see I was being unreasonable, or unpleasant at least. I was something like the stocky old man at the supermarket, still not heeding my own family's advice.

We all seem to disagree a lot these days. Perhaps the one thing people of different beliefs agree on is the existence of this increased disharmony, this rancor, this lack of civility. And yet we can stand in such orderly lines, giving in meekly. To the cost of living, to inevitabilities in an otherwise dangerous world, to getting older. At the same time, there are fewer and fewer things we dare not do.

DEHISCENCE | Forrest Gander

Bursting open   in 1983   John Taggart

published a poem   of capsules fruits anthers   *Dehiscence*

a beauty   to discharge from   Membrane

Press   its mature contents   cracking, releasing

by divergence of parts   the image

locating itself   in a specific field   of the mucous follicles

on Gallows Road   tufts of white hair   Virginia where

into the cavity   of the ovary

traipsed across   an abandoned field   purpletop

and milkweed   gaping pods .   each a theater

for a particular spider   spooked me   the fluff

as   parceling   out of breath

and creamy spittle   on the blades

to this field   or a cut or wound   dissemination

of the afternoon   pale, fat   its front legs raised

yellow   forehead-eye   the pods warty

warm drift of mind   with feather parachutes   lifting away

its publication   of pappus (soft   hairs) demobbed

through fleshy lips the spree of seed   in slightest breeze

going to pieces   breaking up   dismantling the phrase

to begin again to   propagate

the pollen the word   set

free

DIVE | Peggy Shumaker

dive, *n.* span of time under water

Seldom more than an hour at a time—the finite number of our breaths—before divers reach 500 psi and have to surface. We know so little of the vast majority of our world, glimpsed through foggy masks and the twin distortions of sloshing water and broken light.

Worldwide, reefs suffer wherever crown-of-thorns starfish take over. The only creature that finds them delicious and can slip its long foot underneath the crown-of-thorns' formidable armor, flip it, then gorge on the shining delicacies within the star, is this: the Triton's trumpet snail, prized for the dramatic crenulated whorl of its shell. It's prized almost to extinction, its numbers spiraling down, down. And so the crown-of-thorns star munches in a few weeks corals that take decades to grow, corals that shelter nurseries for damselfish, angels, eels, the small fry the rest of the world depends on. In their wake, hungry stars leave acres of skeletons, bleached.

dive, *n.* sleazy bar

E.g., The Boatel, on the south bank of the Chena River, Fairbanks, Alaska, where all summer local drunks minimize their DUIs by firing up their outboards and skimming downriver to the rotting dock. Recently, The Boatel made the paper because it hosted an altercation a little different from the usual bashings and knifings.

In the dank interior, a couple had lost track of how many pitchers they'd downed. They yelled at the TV, "Support our troops, hell yeah. Bring 'em home!"

Two out-of-uniform MPs from Fort Wainwright took exception, with fists. The bouncer shoved the MPs out back, on the deck, the man and woman out front in the parking lot.

The MPs saw the couple's boat, knotted to a piling with nylon rope.

The MPs got in, untied the leaky inflatable, and headed downriver, toward Pike's, away from the reviewing stand where a ceremony soon would be held. Ceremony for them, ceremony for four thousand Stryker Brigade soldiers about to deploy to Iraq. Half of them leaving for the second time or the third. Their commander's voice—"The enemy wants to hurt our country, hurt our families."

> **dive**, *v.* 1. To plunge headfirst into water 2. To plum-
> met, to drop sharply

No one paid Harry to take a dive, just one day his leg muscles didn't hold him up when he put weight on them. Face planted on the patio, quick trip to the ER, and Harry started this long descent into the mysteries of the body. Probing with needles, X-rays, magnetic resonance. No dice. Debilitating, the not knowing.

Back home in his recliner, he flicks on the Beijing Olympics. From the ten-meter platform, the best divers in the world flip three times, twist twice, flatten their hands so the surface opens and closes over them with a tiny feather of splash. Harry and I put together a shower chair so he can, without danger, perform his ablutions. Warm water down his back comforts. Especially when he's not clinging to tiled walls.

I bring home a sturdy walker that fits him, complete with a seat he can sink into when he tires. We store the rickety frame his wife Suzie pushed for two decades, through not knowing, through lupus, through ovarian cancer, through knowing. Tonight it's synchronized events, athletes perfectly attuned, years of daily practice peaking, if they're lucky, into two forms/ one motion. Like the long-married, like Harry and Suzie, their life together never easy. The intense concentration, the consideration of the other, the inevitable plunge.

DOOM | Molly McQuade

The label on the old box read *Doom*. It looked homicidal. It also looked homemade. However, the product was manufactured by the U.S. Department of Agriculture. Stored on the shelf of a tattered New York City streetcorner emporium, *Doom*'s box was small and gray, and the print on the sign of the box was just slightly darker, stepping moderately and deliberately over the sides. No hype.

Directions, numbered, were included on the box, along with general advice and information. Namely, the powder inside was not toxic. And, namely, several seasons of use would have to pass before the desired effects of *Doom* could be felt. Then, more info. Ingredients were listed. But close reading didn't really pay off, since each one was a fairly exotic word. Next came numbered instructions for where to put the powder, and how.

Instruction number one was, "Shake box to fluff up *Doom*."

Doom was supposed to give milky spore disease to Japanese beetles, themselves a blight to any garden. (They would eat almost anything in it.) *Doom* would kill the beetle larvae, helping

65

the garden, for a span of decades. Yet the packaging of *Doom* looked so amateurish, and *Doom* took so long—many beetle life cycles—to accomplish what was needed.

Still, the wording was authoritative. I *wanted* to believe.

"Shake box to fluff up *Doom.*"

The imperative reminded me of Emily Dickinson's writing—her asperity, her brevity, and her occasional lightheadedness. It also reminded me of the well-known T. S. Eliot refrain from his poem "The Love Song of J. Alfred Prufrock": "In the room the women come and go / Talking of Michelangelo." Both refrains, *Doom*'s and Prufrock's, appear to be emblematic of something larger; they are like stray melodies.

But *Doom*'s message is more direct and more pragmatic. The Department of Agriculture seems to be saying, "Heed this." And, however inadvertently, "Take hope." If you would only fluff up your *Doom* just right, then everything should work out fine for you. Won't it? Isn't that so?

Fluffy doom, fluffed up by you: a worthy subject for anyone to mull, a good thing on its own terms. Maybe less daft than it sounds.

Shake it well.

Now and then, the accidental craft of something, like the packaging, wording, and wisdom of *Doom*, leaves an impression—an impression perhaps deeper than what is made in a moment by some intentional art. The unexpected kind of craft, you believe, has no motive, so it must be true. Nature is speaking through matter to you, even if nature's medium is the U.S. government.

The odd mingling of a practical communiqué with the chance eloquence of a word or two can be deeply satisfying. Plants and animals are strays; that's how they survive and thrive. They're generous without meaning to be, and populist in how they spread. The skittering truths of words can stray, too. The proof of their power *is* to stray.

Echo | Rusty Morrison

It's the hour before dawn. I'm at my desk, steadying against the stillness, not writing. In the past few weeks, I've been working to complete a long poem cycle. I could choose to return to writing my way through the small revisions that it needs. But the more courageous move is motionlessness, where I can feel myself breathing, braving the patience that is wide, smooth-surfaced, and steady enough to allow for echo.

I could call this patience a practice of allowing for the lack of echo, as it resonates against other lacks, a kind of tuning fork of un-fixities, which disregards the constant barrage of regular, regulated sound, and which prepares my listening to open itself to some element of past or present that will find the correct acoustics—the correct hardness—to create a resonance in which I might discern pattern and potential, rather than simply hear the past's replicas.

Keeping that kind of openness as the shape of my attention's middle ground means not bracing for event, but being open to absorbing its traces of otherness. Not a return of the past, but a slant-knowing that gives the already-known a quality of the strange, reminding me that any sensory event can become a channel for alternatives, extending what is no longer the past into what is not yet the future.

Probably because *echo* is an idea very close to my process, *echo*, as a word, is difficult for me to use in my poetry. How to bring the rest of the poem's text into accord with the sound-sense continuum of echo's calibrations, so that the poem achieves a resonance I can call worthy of echo's harmonic occlusions and invitations? I find, in my use of the word, either too much of the common measure of the mythic or of the metaphoric, both washed with nostalgia. Not surprisingly, these are failings I struggle with in my poetry, regardless of the words I use.

For an echo to form, there must be hard and stable surfaces; and for the ear to hear an echo, there must be enough delay for the difference to be perceived. A poem must suggest to me that both of these qualities of echo are present. Such beginnings tantalize me with the hope that I might create the proper acoustics to allow each instance's immediacy to differentiate from what came before it, so that I will hear in that difference more than I had thought was possible to perceive.

But just as an echo, if repeated over and over, loses its uncanniness—its beauty is, in part, surprise—so too, if craft methods are repeated too often, their results no longer heighten, or hearken to, immediacy's less obvious offerings.

It is easy to muse about such things in the abstract, but excruciatingly difficult to practice them, especially if writing asks me to be open to a still palpably painful experience. Using the word *echo* in my poems is fraught with challenges, and so is trying to bring the most painful immediacies of my life into my writing practice. In both cases, I am working against stereotypes, against the obscuring tendency of mythologies, as well as against the generalizing call-and-response of the culture's norms, which is mesmerizing—against all the ways in which I perceive myself and make a self from those perceptions.

❖

Last night, I read a piece in *The New York Times* science section describing an experiment in which all of the participants were college students who considered themselves to be socially awkward. All were to recall a painfully embarrassing memory from high school. Half were asked to give the account in first person and half in third person. Interestingly, the participants who told their story in third person tended to rate themselves as having changed significantly in the years since this earlier experience. And, even more surprising, a statistically significant number of these third-person-story participants demonstrated more sociability in a conversation that followed their recounting (this second conversation was held with someone who, unknown to them, was also a clinician and part of the experiment). The article's writer concluded that the third-person perspective allowed subjects to reflect on the meanings of their interactions from a distance, and concluded that this distance allowed a sense of change to be realized by these participants. I can imagine the students who recounted their experiences in third person as participating in a kind of self-echoing. And this self-echoing is more easily heard and understood if there is a distinguishable distance created between the past and the present. In other words, hearing the past as distanced from the present gives one the freedom, in the present, to change the constitution of what "is" the self by separating her from what "was."

Of course, separations from what "was" that are forced upon us can be devastating. We've all suffered our crises of loss, our deaths. My father died almost exactly a year ago. It was a change that defied my previous coping strategies and my sense of how I constituted the continuum in which I felt myself a part. I still catch myself watching for, and listening to, the lack of his presence, which I feel everywhere, so that my experience of everything is subtly changed, charged with this difference. It is an active and engaging presence of absence, one that is still in flux. How do I expand my frame of understanding so that I can hear and then embrace the self I can become if I fully live these alterations of everything I know?

I've found writing poetry to be the surest place to hear and evaluate the quality of that listening. Again, the echo is a help to me. I like to imagine the shape of the word itself, which to my mind resembles two seashells, each with its back to the other, and its opening facing outward. Each syllable of "echo" offers an open, bowl-like vowel sound—the soft *e* of quiet, nearly internalized remark, and the long *o* of outward contact, a sound that will inflect as either answer or question. They meet at the *ch*, a solidity, which becomes the two vowels' shared striking-pad, yet prevents them from meeting.

I think of a poem's place of initiation, and of the landscape where a finished poem resides, as similar to these two vowels. The *ch* of the writing act's immediacy will do justice to both only if it holds the difference between them in full depth and dimensionality. Or I might say "dementia-ality," since what I expect for a time is a dementia, while the poem shifts reality as I previously understood it. But this word-association is not exact because the full meaning of *dementia* includes a loss of memory, and what I am imagining is not an inevitable loss, but rather a freeing of mind from its constraints of past positioning and practice. My desire for this freedom is probably why I write: because I trust that a more vivid, more vital, more multifaceted reality is available, and that the language of the poem is a means to its realization. I would like to think of this practice as creating an "echo-nomy" in which my listening, in all of its motionless attention, is an attunement to a flow that is larger than—and still encompasses—my understanding, one that passes through a double-blind mirror to appear to me. It is a flow in which the reverberations of as-yet-unseen revelations remain available in any experience, and all past—whether it is just my last pulse-beat or a decades-old memory—is, in its own way, as filled with possibility as all future. Of course, if my writing does not create its own echo, if it is too soft acoustically, too reflective of habit's manner and guise, too easily taken up with my typical modes of perceiving, then the soundings have not entered the economy I am after. More silence. More listening needed.

EEK | Daina Lyn Galante

"That girl is always eeking!"

"Oh, I friggin' know. She's so annoying. I hate that she does that obnoxious hand-lifting thing, like she's some kind of cat. Her voice goes right through me. She eeks me out."

"Honestly, everything eeks you out, though."

"That's true. Eeking eeks me."

To *eek* is to act out the word and/or the feeling of being disgusted. It's the verb for one's reaction to something hideous, ridiculous, and sickening. For an example of whom to eek at, an ex-boyfriend's new girlfriend is definitely worthy of an eek.

One may ask: How does one properly eek?

In order to really push the point that he/she is completely turned off, one must raise the hands to approximately shoulder-height in a clawlike clench. Then the face must follow suit by scrunching the nose and mouth. The emotion in the eyes will show on its own. One must look horrified. Then, when the face-hand coordination is perfect, one must make the eeking noise. He/she has to make sure to elaborate on the long *e* sound. This is key when eeking.

One can be eeked. This is usually referred to as being "eeked out."

To be eeked, a person feels appalled by the situation at hand. Simple things can eek a person, such as sitting in gum and then having to touch the unknown chewer's leavings, or the way the subway smells. However, a person can become eeked by more intricate experiences and things. Some of these would include the way people talk, act, eat, look, and feel.

Some have suggested that the term *eeked out* is synonymous with the term *grossed out*. However, one cannot gross. One can eek, though.

Tenses of the verb *eek*:

Past. "You used to eek all the time when your roommate threw up immediately after the keg stand. You haven't eeked at all, lately; you must have just gotten used to the smell."

Present. "Who are you eeking at? I will come over there and smack you right across your face if you eek at me again."

Future. "I think I need to eek at this kid. All day he has been picking his nose. Yeah, I will eek at him in a minute."

In rare cases: "She is such an eeking little b****!" (Again, a reference to the ex-boyfriend's new girlfriend.)

EYE | Katherine Vaz

EYE: eye. How many words draw for us what they are? The *e* and *e* are our eyes, the *y* is the hook of our nose and mouth. Red, yellow, and blue make all the colors under our gaze. Lavender smells sweet; the scent comes through your eyes before it enters your nose. The eye of memory.

I had eye surgery twice as a child and can conjure up the ghastly smell of ether. I saw the jelly of the back of my eyes splayed on the walls of the optometrist's office when he shone a light into them: branches of veins that made a forest of my insides on his wall.

A boy I loved in college was dancing with someone else. I left the room and came back because I couldn't believe it, but my eyes saw it again; they have always been ahead of my mind.

Cataracts in old age—one day I learned that the word also means "waterfall." Lashes. Lids. Iris. Lids painted brown, gold, and mauve. Pink glasses. We hold panes to our eyes.

The optic nerve is blind. We see, in fact, in lace, with dots of blindness that are covered by the swiftness of the eye. Our eyesight enters us through a tube that has no sight. What does it mean to have someone look into our eyes and see himself upside down? What does it mean to look into someone and see ourselves captured whole but small?

I, I, I, I, the implacable.

My love's eyes are blue. Mine are green. I gave him a tie striped with these shades and he gave me a recording of "In Your Eyes." There's a fable from the Azores I learned as a child: One day a shepherd with blue eyes fell in love with a princess with green eyes, but they could not be together, so they wept. A blue lake poured from his eyes, and a green lake from hers. He jumped into the lake of her eyes and drowned; she drowned in his, too. They rest beside each other now.

"Ai, ai, ai," my grandmother used to sigh when life was rough (she uttered this often, she sank heavily into chairs; we used to imitate her, laughing). *Ai*—the dying man's final word is supposed to be printed upon the soft lip of the hyacinth.

The pathways of our lives—where our vision has led us— draw an infrared line that marks the world, the way police will outline in chalk where a body lies. The design is visible from above, I like to think: wild looping and petals, long projectiles, dots, stillness, and outline upon outline when we hold someone.

What do these pictures look like from the heavens? I wonder if this is why God does not seem to answer us, because He is staring amazed at the near whiteout of what we have seen clear to create, how we have moved, and He is saying, "If only you could see this unfold as I do, God's-eye, how beautiful you are."

FACT | Srikanth Reddy

The tomb of Dante in Florence lies empty. The
cosmos is shaped like a saddle of stars. I close my
book and look out the window. A whale floats by
clicking. Pyramids crumble beyond the horizon.
My book says the world divides into facts. Under
the rail bridge a couple drinks champagne and
orange juice from plastic flutes dug out of a basket.
Moreover the book says we make to ourselves
pictures of facts. I picture the War of the Spanish
Succession. In the foreground a man in a
powdered wig waves a broken cutlass. His men
pour out of a boat full of smoke. Once there was a
little boy who slept in the sand with arms folded.
The picture is a model of reality. When he woke
the ocean was closer.

FELT | Annie Finch

Felt blend felt heavy felt ancient felt touched felt given felt fiber felt wool felt weave felt made felt blended felt massaged felt changed felt touched felt given felt heft felt driven felt hung felt moved felt stroked felt fed felt hugged felt much felt soft felt move felt fiber felt water felt earth felt touched felt held felt slept felt known felt spelled

FIASCO | Wendy Rawlings

Fiasco sounds robustly Italian, as do many of the words that have migrated from Italy to America as this one has, coming from the word for *flask*. I like to imagine the small, flat, bad-boy flask for liquor that advertising men in the sixties kept in their desks for a nip. So I was disappointed to find the Italian *fiasco* refers instead to the squat, straw-wrapped bottles that, in the family-style Italian restaurants of my childhood—Stango's, Pizza Delicious—were lined up along the walls, for decoration, after being drained of their cheap Chianti.

The Italian phrase *far fiasco* means literally "to make a bottle," which means figuratively "to fail in a performance." Some linguists speculate the word first came into use based on errors Italian actors made on the eighteenth-century French stage. I've always liked the way *fiasco* contains an emphatic, hidden *ass* that, when spoken by Americans, you can hear but not see. As a flask is a misshapen bottle, a fiasco is a human effort gone wrong, making asses of us.

One summer, I taught in a study-abroad program in Italy with an American couple, both Renaissance scholars, whose sartorial choices tended toward the theatrical. He favored a goatee and ponytail to accent crushed-velvet vests and frock coats, wide-sleeved shirts with a ruffle or flounce, and black boots with big buckles that made him, a Shakespeare geek from Kansas, look like a pretty good mock-up of a pirate. She wore dangly earrings, crushed-velvet skirts, peasant blouses, and a gold armlet in the shape of an asp. This gypsy wench was a fan of cheap jug wine and liked to smoke cigarettes in a long holder. Somehow, this couple's theatricality and the hassle of chaperoning thirty unseasoned undergraduates around Italy meant they created a fiasco wherever they went.

Each morning as we gathered outside the Italian language school, our students complained vociferously about their homestay arrangements. They had to sleep on the floor, they were allowed only one shower a week, there was far too much food, or too little. One student shut everyone up when she announced that for breakfast she'd been served nothing but a raw egg. Still, my colleagues were unmoved by such a display. "Spoiled rich kids," they would sneer out of the sides of their mouths.

I shouldn't say they were unmoved entirely. Theatrical people live for this kind of stuff. Leaving Venice by train, I looked up to see my colleagues wearing Venetian carnival masks with long beaked noses, Pulcinella and El Diavolo. Here we go again, I thought.

My own family was too non-confrontational to get whipped up into the kind of frenzy that precipitates a fiasco. Blow-ups were averted by someone (me) slamming the bedroom door, or pouring herself a glass of wine (my mother), or going out to the garage to work on the car (my father). The worst altercation I'd ever seen, until I was old enough to get dropped off at the movie theater, was Lucy and Ricky arguing over her purchase of too many hats on *I Love Lucy*.

Years later, when my parents' marriage was tanking, my mother started spending a lot of time with a woman she'd met at work. Jan (I'll call her) weighed more than 300 pounds and favored men's polo shirts and khaki pants. She was a rabid Yankees fan, an insomniac who needle-pointed flowers on pillowcases late into the night, and she was in love with my mother. My parents divorced, and my mother and Jan moved in together, got a white lapdog who liked to perch on Jan's wide upper arm, and cultivated new friends, such as the couple named Donna and Donna. I couldn't find a way to explain the transfer of my mother's affections from my serious, coat-and-tie-wearing father to a 350-pound woman. Every stable institution now seemed to teeter on an unsteady foundation.

That year, I nose-dived into my first major depression. Someone recommended Rapid Eye Therapy, so once a week for several months I sat in a La-Z-Boy recliner while a woman knelt in front of me and waved a bright-tipped wand, reciting an inventory of negative thoughts and feelings from which I would be neurologically cleansed. One day I began to cry during treatment.

"Why are you crying?" she asked.

"Isn't that what I'm supposed to do in therapy?"

"Crying's just a way of discharging pent-up energy," she said. "Really, laughing's a lot more effective."

Toward the end of my treatment, my Rapid Eye therapist told me she'd grown up in a Mormon family with eight siblings. On her birthday every year, one of her older sisters would always give her extra attention and a far better gift than anyone else. When she was sixteen, she learned that this sister was actually her mother. Pregnant out of wedlock when she herself was sixteen, and threatened with the prospect of disgracing her family, my therapist's mother had agreed to an arrangement whereby her child was raised as her youngest sibling. Since discovering this, my Rapid Eye therapist had left the Mormon church for Reiki, Rapid Eye Therapy, and a champion chess-playing girlfriend.

According to the Online Etymology Dictionary, an Italian dictionary cites the phrase *fare il fiasco* as meaning "to play a game so that one that loses will pay for the fiasco." But as one might expect, losing simply means buying the next bottle of wine. Another Italian anecdote has it that Venetian glassmakers on the island of Murano tossed aside imperfect pieces to be made into common flasks. Whether either of these excavated bits of etymological history has any grounding in truth, they both convey the spirit of the word *fiasco*. Fiascoes, happily, aren't much more to fuss over than badly-made bottles, a far cry from catastrophes.

Yet when I mentioned to a friend that I was writing about the word *fiasco*, he said that of course I'd have to mention Tom Ricks's book, *FIASCO: The American Military Adventure in Iraq*. Sure enough, the first clause of the first Amazon review of the book refers to the "more strongly worded title that you might expect a seasoned military reporter . . . to use." I agree that *fiasco* is a surprise, because it doesn't seem to have enough gravitas to describe an unprecedented and unprovoked invasion of another country. Rather, *fiasco*, like its sisters *blunder* and *bungle*, is one of those words for screw-ups on a much smaller scale.

For me, *fiasco* connotes a wingdings-for-curse-words kind of universe, where slapstick and pratfalls reign and problems can be solved with beer and hugs. In my favorite scene from *Husbands and Wives*, Juliette Lewis, as Woody Allen's student, leaves her teacher's only copy of his novel manuscript in a New York City cab. He gets the manuscript back. When I hear *fiasco* in my head, the inflection is always Woody Allen's agitated, stuttering whine.

To wit: our fiascoes were supposed to take place on the small stage and be forgotten over a bottle of Chianti, not blow people to bits in a very bad war.

FILTHY | Marilyn Krysl

"These are filthy," my mother said in 1946.

She tossed my father's bloody slaughterhouse clothes into the wash. We lived in prairie country where earth—its soil, which I thought of as dirt—was the dominant fact. *Filthy*: the word meant really dirty, soiling something my mother would have to scrub by hand, and hard. I went outside to my chipped basin in which I mixed dirt with water, and made mud figures, one female, one male: Adam and Eve. I made mud pies to feed them, whispering the word *filthy*, feeling with my mouth the fricative *f*, the long purl of the *l*, the quick stop of the *y*. "Filthy," I crooned over my mud, this goopy, good, filthy malleability.

I knew mud made things filthy, but I did not experience mud as dirty. Mud had texture I liked to feel with my hands. Mud, made of water and dirt, the world's basic ingredients. Even people were made from it. "For dust thou art," my grandmother's Bible said, "and unto dust thou shalt return."

Everything was made of filthy mud, and so could not be bad. "Wonderful mud," I crooned, good, filthy mud.

❖

There is pleasure in ablution, the pleasure of feeling clean. A bath, and I'm reborn. Then slowly my body wears through time, and at some point I have accumulated—or evolved into—rankness. I'm filthy. But being filthy sometimes feels pleasant. In the garden, weary and elated with the pleasure of having worked hard digging and lifting shovelfuls of soil, my every pore feels opened and emptied out with effort. The caul of sweat and dirt on my skin feels like an earned blessing. I've come through the ceremony of hard labor, and now the word *filthy* rises up, but—how can this be?—it means its opposite. I'm fully filthy in the best possible way. The word *filthy* has become celebratory.

My mother lived in the era of public toilets' paper shields. Even if I was desperate, she insisted on placing the shield on the seat.

"These seats are filthy. We don't know who sat here."

The world housed people who seldom bathed. They lacked "good sense" and sat on public toilets without a thought for the welfare of others.

Who were these people?

"Vagrants," she said.

Vagrants were people who didn't bathe and had no money. She made me walk past them quickly. The filthy, she believed, carried diseases. She, a mother with the best intentions who would protect me from even the word *filthy*.

Filth: the polite deny it, the fastidious decry it, and the well-off hire help to disappear it. Though even the modern aristocrat wipes his own ass and so must notice this congress with his own filth. Let's hope the experience humbles him. Feces are perceived as dirty, but at the same time feces are ordinary, necessary, humble, and ubiquitous as breath. Bottom-basic. The body cannot choose not to deliver its daily filth—teeth, hair, the flaking off of thousands of bits of skin—and feces.

I had seen animals eat feces, and behold, in those moments filth was food—like the mud pies my Adam and Eve ate instead of an apple.

❖

Filth, n. (ME, *filthe, fulthe, felthe;* AS *fylthe* base of *ful*). 1. Foul dirt; disgusting matter. 2. Feces. 3. Moral corruption or something causing it; indecency; obscenity. We are in the toilet here, literally and figuratively, and foul are filthy feces. *Filthy* is a word firmly yoked to its meaning, so why in my consciousness does it morph? Because to perceive the word *filthy* in another way, as a kind of beauty, is a way of defying my mother's insistence on protecting me from the world I had to live in? Or is this morphing of the word merely joyful semantic play in which I defy the powerful literal? As in sitting at the piano naked, playing and singing "Onward Christian Soldiers"?

I sense another motive. See *foul*, Webster's suggests. *Foul* is Middle English and Anglo-Saxon, and is also akin to German's *faul*, meaning "rotten, putrid, lazy."

Lazy?

Here is the link between the word *filthy* and the people my mother called vagrants. The word *filthy* lies cheek by jowl with poverty.

I knew the poor were different from us. They had less money. Then I was ten, and a case of the mumps left me permanently deaf in my left ear. My mother, intending sympathy, said, "You poor thing." An image rose of me in ragged clothes, no money, starving. For this reason I became curious about the poor.

At Christmas we filled sacks with groceries, but the church distributed the sacks, so we didn't see the people who received them. How, I wondered, had they become poor?

Everyone gave the same answer: they'd failed to practice frugality.

"Back in the old country our family was poor," my father said. "Your grandparents were peasants working for the landlord. But now we're better off, because we work hard and save." He went along with my mother's insistence we buy new furniture. But when I gave my new sweater to Marlene in a burst of wanton generosity, my parents told me that I was not to squander its bright red wool by giving it away.

Distinctions blazed: the poor might get drunk, but we stayed sober. They might have "diseases." We did not. Beneath these distinctions lay the unspoken assumption that Americans were self-reliant people who went into business and prospered. Those who did not prosper had failed to pull themselves up by their bootstraps. They were, in effect, lazy. Not only were the poor destitute, due to their laziness they were also un-American.

Their condition was shameful.

The tautology was crazy-making: the poor became repositories of shame because it was shameful to be poor.

Now I understand that when my mother declared a person or thing filthy, she invoked her worst fear: if we did not keep ourselves spanking clean, we would fall into poverty and become destitute—without even a bathtub or a toilet of our own.

❖

The poor may be penniless in the realm of material wealth, but according to the Beatitudes another level applies. "Blessed are the poor in spirit," the first Beatitude says, "for theirs is the kingdom of heaven." What does it mean to be poor in spirit? It means to feel like one has no spirit left, and to feel scared, cast out, and ashamed. These then are the people who will have it made in the afterlife. They will wear my word *filthy* in joy.

❖

A friend in a hurry tracks mud across my kitchen floor. I get down on my knees and scrub. The connotation of *filthy* is negative, but as I scrub, the word *filthy* meshes with my scrubbing, and now, slowly, the word fills with an overflowing sensuality. I'm one with my labor, and as I pay close attention, I notice that every cell of me is present, throbbing. This heightening of my senses makes the word *filthy* suggest the rich muck which makes sumptuous gardens. I go on scrubbing and now I'm humming the word *filthy*. See me crooning and scrubbing. Time goes on, and slowly the word—and also the floor—becomes more and more sweetly clean.

I feel the way I feel after a bath, when I towel off and rise a little into the air. The floor is clean, and I feel wonderfully filthy.

I'm filthy rich, and I would share this word's largesse.

May I be filthy, may you be filthy. May all living beings be filthy.

❖

Filthy slides in and out of its literal meaning as though definition is clothing, and my lover undresses me, kisses my belly, and banters.

"Oh, you are so filthy!" he says, meaning that I please him greatly.

Filthy won't lie still. It rises up and insists on itself as worthy. It demands equal opportunity with beauty. St. Paul doesn't approve, but *filthy* doesn't care. It's going to dance naked whenever it wants. It wants to move, to morph, to be here and then gone, shimmer of light across silk—and at the same time it wants to be resoundingly foul. *Filthy* wants it both ways. It would defy the binary bind. Like the yin-yang nestled against each other's curves, the word would transcend all oppositional dead ends. It insists on embodying transcendence.

❖

Today I am riding a bus in the direction of the Homeless Shelter, and my mother's voice sits on my shoulder. A man gets on. His jeans are stiff with grime. His shirt's dirty, torn, and he smells sweaty. *Rank,* says my mother's voice. *Filthy.*

He has only coins, not enough for the fare, so another rider gives him the difference. You might say I'm privileged—I have a bus pass, and he doesn't—but on the momentary human level this fact neither damns me nor exalts him. He sits beside me. There we are, wearing our bodies. Genealogical attire. Our skin is outerwear, and on his forehead is a smudge. Dirt under his fingernails. Maybe he has worked construction today, or landscaping. I don't know if he feels himself a failure at this moment or if he's proud of how he's negotiating the day. He's another human citizen, and we all live in bodies in various states of filthiness. In those moments I perceive him as filthy in my sense of the word—a word filled to the brim with the body's beauty.

He sits in the silence of his body, a body quietly singing its song of filth. A hymn.

❖

Is it only I who experience the word *filthy* as sublime?

Imagine many of us, a great crowd filling the streets of the metropolis, bodies pouring into the central avenue, a great crowd becoming more crowded with more humans, humans attired in the body's enclosing and flaking skin, and all of those bodies shouting in unison, shouting *filthy* with vigor, mouthing it with lips' and tongues' bodily joy, all of us high on a single word's transformation, shouting *filthy* like an anthem of the human. The word *filthy* shriven of its negative, literal meaning, a word become blessed.

FLOCCINAUCINIHILIPILIFICATION

Siobhan Gordon

Floccinaucinihilipilification, the noun, is a favorite of mine. The word literally means "the estimation of something as valueless" (dictionary.com). It has even been used as a synonym for "nothing." An example my father once gave me in order to explain its meaning is, "I'm very sorry that my floccinaucinihilipilification of the history of the poodle bothers you so much, but it just doesn't at all interest me." Quite obviously, this word is not used in everyday conversation. It is most known for being one of the longest words in the English language—even longer than *antidisestablishmentarianism,* which many people claim is the longest word.

My father uses *floccinaucinihilipilification* all too frequently. He loves to try to stick it into his everyday conversation. Granted, most people just stare at him in bewilderment when he does, but I do believe that's the reason he uses it. Even North Carolina Senator and Foreign Relations Committee Chairman Jesse Helms used it on July 20, 1999, during the ratification process of the Comprehensive Test Ban Treaty, or CTBT. Helms was opposed to the ratification and said in response to forty-five

Democrats pleading with him to allow hearings on the treaty, "I note your distress at my floccinaucinihilipilification of the CTBT [but] I do not share your enthusiasm for this treaty for a variety of reasons."

When I use *floccinaucinihilipilification*, I don't even put it in real sentences. I simply say it for pleasure. For example, when there's a lull in the conversation, or if things have been quiet for too long, I'll say it to fill up the silence. Saying it is actually a lot of fun, when you've finally learned how. Go on, try it! Out loud, silly. Now, isn't that just delightful?

Floccinaucinihilipilification is sometimes said to have been created by an extremely bored student of Eton College in the mid-eighteenth century. This young man apparently found four different ways of saying "nothing" when flipping through his Eton Latin Grammar textbook and simply fused them. In Latin, *flocci non facere* means "to not give a hoot about"; *naucum* means "something very small," and *non nauci habere* means "to think nothing of"; *nihil* means "nothing," and *nihili facere* means "to consider as worthless"; *pilus* means "a trifle," and *non pili facere* means "to care not a whit for."

The creator of *floccinaucinihilipilification* may have thought it comical that there were so many words that meant "nothing" in his Latin textbook. Therefore, he strung them together to make one very misleadingly long and complicated word. Upon first hearing this word, one might think that its definition would be something tricky, but it's not. Ironically, this deceptive word means "nothing." Down the line, people began using it in serious situations, but it started its existence as a joke.

FLORERE | Vincent Katz

As poets, we have accessible to us all the valences of given words. A word is not a definable, mute object, but a complex mechanism, capable of multiple extensions that can be elicited by the poet depending largely on its combinations with other words. Activations of a word's potentials are determined by the other words with which it is combined and also by the manner in which words are connected.

My plan is to study as deeply as I can the potentials of as many English words as possible, in order to develop greater poetic flexibility. I have studied Ancient Greek, Latin, French, Italian, Portuguese, and Spanish, partly as avenues into cultures using those languages, partly to gain greater knowledge of my own language, English, as those languages have played roles in its development.

Here, I would like to lay a groundwork to explain the usage of a single word in a single poem of mine—the Latin *florere*, familiar to English readers in the form *floruit*, "was in her/ his prime." I do not actually use the word but rather some of its definitions. They are there to be recognized in the poem, if one's ear is attuned to the sounds of different languages echoing in our multicultural, multi-epochal communal space.

❖

During 1998, I was working on a long poem, "Painted Life," whose method included writing so fast that there was little chance of conscious second-guessing, enabling a greater reliance on internal music, sounds I would hear in my head. I learned from "Painted Life" that words can combine into poetry without syntax and also that, even when the conscious decision maker is sent to the sidelines, meaning is embedded in words by nature. The detonations that occur when one word is simply placed next to another are complex and not entirely predictable.

In September 1998, in São Paulo, Brazil, I wrote three poems: "Breads and Sweets," "Beleaguered Few," and "Rapid Departures." "Beleaguered Few" is an example of my most unapologetically "musical" style: the word choices were governed almost completely by sound. If the sound I heard did not correspond to an actual English word, I would invent a word to fit the sound, though only as a last resort. Likewise, if I could not find an English word to correspond to a given sound, I might try another language—Portuguese, perhaps, or, since I was then immersed in the poetry of Sextus Propertius, his native tongue, Latin.

"Beleaguered Few" begins by using real English words in willfully opaque juxtapositions:

> only wet-throughs rescind
> abstract mention pip
> inside overgone ripple
> pledge a vice Porsche

Soon, the sounds require the verse to move beyond English to a flurry of invented "English" mixed with Latin:

> prenostic enticity
> spirum robst spungit
> ensiculus peritus
> volens flamma refert

When I published the poem in the book *Rapid Departures*, I provided a "translation" of these last three lines: "the skillful dagger / penetrates the coil / the willing flame recalls." This is Latin that came from my head. I am interested in attempting to write real Latin, but I am just as interested in inventing Latin. It gives me the feeling of creating a spoken, personal language, like the ones people use all the time every day, which do not stay within the confines of textbook grammar and syntax. They also do not stay within the realms of received vocabulary, and neither does mine. After the Latin outburst, the poem returns to oddly juxtaposed English words for its conclusion, one of its characteristics being the creation of hyphenated words. "Side-travel" seems now to me to be an apt name for how this poem works:

> reverting to side-travel
> hinged, hinting procure
> consultory present said
> fore-cease tendered tied

"Beleaguered Few" presaged in microcosm the poem "Rapid Departures," which I dedicated to Augusto de Campos, master of the musical word-unit and one of the founders of the Poundian Noigandres group based in São Paulo, that helped establish Concrete Poetry in Brazil in the early 1950s. "Rapid Departures" extends "Beleaguered Few"'s procedures to attempt a large-scale musical statement. At ten pages, it is long enough to allow different poetic (and prosaic) tendencies to flow in and out. There are intermittent logical flows in the poem, but they do not amount to logical conclusions; rather, they are spurts of logic, or narrative, that, by their inconclusiveness, exhibit a oneness with flows of nonlogical, asyntactic phrases.

This pattern of interweaving languages establishes an environment in which the reader may expect to find the search for music abandoning the ship of standard English. There are hints this will occur on the poem's first page ("attuned / breaks / in syntax"). Then, as in "Beleaguered Few," strange forms ("Lizbeth," "cicatrice") and hyphenations ("Graham-switch") appear. Soon one finds "corpus salutum," which seems like it might mean "healthy body," except that would be "corpus sanum" (as in *orandum est ut sit mens sana in corpore sano*, "a healthy body and healthy mind are most to be prayed for," Juvenal, 10.356). The *mens* of "Rapid Departures" is not one I would characterize as healthy; it is rather an unquiet one, whose search has a decidedly corporal twist. By the time one comes upon "canicula improcera," which might be translated as "little bitch," it seems likely that a disturbed state ("improcera" can suggest "improper" to an English reader) is driving this poetic.

Just after the aforementioned undersized female canine, about halfway through the poem, come the following lines:

> to bloom, to be in one's
> prime, to foam, ferment
> be eminent, abound in
> swarm with . . .

This seems happy as poetry, for the ideas and simultaneous music in which they are clothed. It also happens to come directly from a particular dictionary, edited to make it musical. The dictionary in question is *The New College Latin & English Dictionary* by John C. Traupman, Ph.D., copyright 1966 by Bantam Books,

Inc., New York, 12th printing (after August, 1971), the same volume I had while in school in the 1970s and which traveled with me from New York to Brazil and back again, and which is here with me now in New York in 2007.

In this essay I have chosen to write about a Latin word defined by the words in the above-quoted stanza. That much was easy; more difficult was to rediscover the Latin source word. I searched through many more "professional," less "collegiate," dictionaries. Soon, I realized the word I sought was *florere*, but I needed to find again the precise wordings of those definitions. Finally, my search led me back to *The New College Latin & English Dictionary*, where I found again the comfort of those particular phrases. I recognized every dictionary has its own tone, its own language—and its own value.

As "Rapid Departures" moves toward its conclusion, one notices the attempt to give measure to the "insane whip" of its unhealthy mind. In a poem that, for most of its length, was composed of bursts as opposed to stanzas, a section of seven five-line stanzas indicates a desire to give form to the inchoate. Just before the end, there is a section of five four-line stanzas in which, despite the claim that "a calm vent has arisen," the insanity of word-collisions swells one last time, and "your mind trickles down / you are left standing /. . . you are left with pale tentacles / braziers tepid in return vaults / unbidden. . . ."

The poem's final stanza attempts to come to terms with the strange reckonings that have occurred—the conflict between body and mind or the *mens insana in corpore insano*—and to come to terms with the delving into Latin, which have brought the worlds of mythology and psychology into play. Those powers control our loves and lives and must be respected. Disrespected, they will come back to disturb us:

I think I've found a way of fitting it all in
I like to be ahead of myself, ahead of the poem

raucous laughter diminishing at length
I believe in the gods
and I'm hoping it works out

The definitions of *florere* I found and composed into poetry form the central, hopeful moment of "Rapid Departures"'s record of unstable mental states. They imply an ever-possible rebirth.

In a high-school class on Greek tragedy, our teacher asked us if we believed everyone's life forms an arc with one highest point. A Greek boy answered, "Yes, of course. You are a child, then you grow into a powerful adult, then you decline." Schooled in the thinking of Carlos Castaneda, I thought no, life is an ever-unfolding possibility. Even in the midst of physical decline—which can occur from deprivation as much as from age—I believe the mind can continue to learn. Even if the mind itself turns a corner, the spirit, if nurtured, can continue to be vibrant. I believe that, at any moment in one's life, it is possible to access the reality of: "to bloom, to be in one's / prime, to foam, ferment / be eminent, abound in / swarm with. . . ." "Rapid Departures"'s ending is tentative ("I think . . . I like . . . I believe . . . I'm hoping . . ."), probably in deference to another Greek belief—that we cannot see the future and thus can count no person happy until we know her or his end. Yet, I have the courage to write another poem, whose ending will not be tentative, whose embrace of the immediate will be unmitigated, if only I can find the words to unlock it.

FORGET | Mimi Schwartz

Just don't forget to. . . !
—what Mother always said

True, you don't want to forget the teapot on the stove, the one
that never seems to whistle reliably as water boils to nothing.
Or the oatmeal that crusts into permanency if you forget it's
cooking while you take a bath. Or the names of things, like
birds of the Galapagos you watched so carefully ten years ago,
especially the one that sounds like breasts and stands on one
foot, Bobos something. Or whoever told you about that great
new restaurant in Soho last week, a really great place, something
Pot or was it Kettle? Or was it at the South Street Seaport? Could
be, and if you remembered who told you, you could call.

Not that you're concerned (unless the house burns down).
Look, even the nineteen-year-old in the Yankees cap yesterday
forgets things—and not just to wear a jacket when it snows.
He couldn't remember the name of his course or its teacher.
"Gee, Mr. S something." You didn't try to jog his memory with
questions about readings, sure that if he signs up to take the

course again, he'll be fine. As you were fine, when you were listening to disk three of *Jude the Obscure* and realized that you'd heard it last year. It didn't matter because you were hooked again, ready to find out what will happen to Jude and Sue Bridehead looking for love in Christown or Christminster.

❖

The palest ink is better than the best memory.

—Chinese proverb

Oatmeal, macaroni and cheese, OJ with pulp. As a bride being efficient, I started with shopping lists: *Call the Gutter Man . . . Send "Meatloaf in the Freezer" essay to* Ms. Magazine *. . . Buy a fifty-foot garden hose holder . . .* got sorted onto separate pages, imposing structure on a scattered life. I usually misplaced the lists, but writing them got the muddle out of my head, most days.

Same with the journals I kept until that summer night when I reread them and got disgusted. Whine, whine, whine about being misunderstood, sad, undervalued, unrecognized—except when I thought I was the luckiest, happiest person in the world. They all went in the dumpster along with whoever it was wrote them. Or so I thought until I cleaned out a closet last week, and there She was again, in three notebooks in an unmarked carton:

> Today I'm 45. Happy Birthday to me. Do I feel my age? What does that mean? When I was 15, 45 seemed nearer the end of life. At 25, it still seemed pretty old. But I feel young, with many options open, and I feel more confidence to take them.

This woman is so upbeat, not at all the one I remembered—and we totally agree about this age business. Ever since I turned sixty-five, seventy is young, as I told my glum friend yesterday.

It was her big 7-O birthday and we were on the tennis courts. "Don't forget you just beat me!" I said while trying to remember that I still beat a friend who is forty-eight.

There were also entries that loved a trip to Egypt, and ranted about Tolstoy's "All happy families are alike," and one I couldn't believe:

> I'm afraid of cancer—creeping on my skin, under my skin, gathering into a silent mass in some dark corner of myself. But they say you can avoid it by thinking positive, imagining everything lit up by light bulbs, white blood cells blinding the malignancies with their luster. . . .

This woman was a Cassandra, writing this entry two years before the doctor found the lump. How did she know—and how did I forget her knowing? Over the years, it seems as if I had saved only a sliver of self, the one I least wanted to remember. The others, whom I liked much more, would have been erased and out of the story if I hadn't, luckily, stashed them away instead of throwing them away. I felt as I did when I found the old photo of me in high school with a pageboy of auburn hair, kneeling on the grass in plaid Bermuda shorts, and deciding, "*You* look better than *I* thought."

❖

Memory is the diary that chronicles things that never have happened. . . .

—Oscar Wilde

We were doing the Lindy at the junior prom, and he landed hard on my foot because he miscalculated or I got the move wrong. "Forget it!" I said easily, but years later I still feel his whomp on my black heels. And then I took my shoes off, in trust, and danced wildly in stocking feet under strobe lights spinning in reds and blues. No, I don't exactly remember that, but I can feel the cool dance floor below me and the freedom of flinging my shoes under the table for a long, beautiful night.

Much later there is the green Dodge skidding on ice across the divided road, spinning me full circle into the phone pole backward. The seat broke, taking the impact, and that's why I walked away without a scratch. It should be my good fortune that overwhelms memory, but no, it's the freedom of spinning I can't forget, of not being in charge, of letting go—until thirty seconds last forever.

❖

Forgive and Forget
        —the sign in Miss Knobbe's class

It was on the wall in third grade, next to *Be Kind,* and *Do Unto Others As You Would Have Them Do Unto You.* Three signs on how to behave, be a good person, get along. *Forgive and Forget,* remembered in red, was the boldest. It totally worked when Arlene spilled apple juice on my homework, but I had some doubts when Johnny took my pencil and stabbed me with it. He liked me, true, and wanted my attention, but my skin still turned blue. And then Arlene and Paula went for an ice-cream sundae without me, said they were sorry when I found out, and next time I went with them. So it did make sense to forgive and forget, but it also made sense to remember.

In my father's village in Germany, the plaque is on the former synagogue, now the Protestant Evangelical Church: *Zur Errinerung und Mahnung* ("As a Reminder and Warning"). It says: "We remember our fellow Jewish citizens who were victims of the Nazi terror regime and those who lost their home."

I am glad it's there, one of many efforts by the villagers not to forget the hard lessons of the Nazi past. The man who takes me around, Herr Stolle, was a teenage soldier in Hitler's army, "an aerial photographer in France." Now, in retirement, he has spent ten years documenting the history of his former Jewish neighbors. He gives me a packet of my family's past here: handwritten insurance records, tax receipts from 1894, a family tree going back to 1750; photographs of the gravestones of grandparents and great-grandparents in the old Jewish cemetery deep in the woods. I am moved by his efforts, a decent man, I feel. He has arranged a visit into my grandfather's house; he escorts me to my ancestral graves, and then his wife serves me home-baked linzer torte. Half-guilty, half-pleased, I sit before a large picture window in 2008, looking out at the red rooftops of a village that now has no Jews, and struggle with how much I can forgive and forget.

❖

Nothing fixes a thing so intensely in memory as the wish to forget it.
                                        —Montaigne

Forget the twinge below the rib when you twist in the bathtub, not every time, mind you. And the *what ifs* of a growth, getting bigger and bigger, until you finally go to the doctor who does all the tests while you worry about cancer, surgery, funerals, and all that you haven't yet done (and all you have done that won't matter) until you hear, "It is nothing. Forget about it!" And you do until, what? Another twist? Another twinge?

Forget the scar you almost had tattooed, now whitish with just a hint of angry red across your chest. The tattoo—a vine with red petals—was meant to say, "So what?" to old definitions of beauty, the ones you grew up on, wearing tight angora sweaters to Foxy's bowling alley, your breasts bigger than Arlene Baker's. The pain of the knife, the raw wound wrapped under stiff gauze, that's long gone, but the phantom left breast keeps returning in the night mirror, a soft milky white.

Forget your mother's last year, and the fury of your "Mom" or "Mother" that proved you were no longer the good daughter. Because she was no longer the mother with the bright smile framed on her dresser, confident and stylish in her red satin dress with hair so thick and black. And so reasonable then, before her eyes and memory failed, before her hair became wisps of gray and she stopped listening to good advice, before the day when you had to identify her in the coffin, face up, rigid, an unrelenting someone you didn't know, even as you nodded, "Yes, that's her."

GRAY | William Corbett

Gray, not with an *e,* because *grey* is not gray to me. I have always responded strongly to weather, and many of my poems and the very impulse to write have begun in the way a day looks and feels. I have lived in Boston since 1964 and in New England most of my life. A gray day, especially a wintry day, but clouded-over, socked-in gray in any season, is a comfort. The rightness of the way it feels is in the word *gray* itself.

Gray also means emotionally gray. Not the blues or sunk in gloom, but a certain melancholy that assists the imagination toward deep concentration.

Shades of gray? Yes, in the sense of acknowledging that there are times when you have to have it both ways, that, for example, Ezra Pound is both a fascist, with all that implies, and a great poet.

As a boy I read the Landmark Series biographies and thought Stonewall Jackson and Robert E. Lee more heroic than William Tecumseh Sherman and Ulysses S. Grant. That the Confederacy was a lost cause may have helped. When I entered middle age, I didn't reach for Grecian Formula to hide my gray hairs. But gray uniforms and a head of gray hair are not in the word, not consciously, when I use it. Instead I feel the soft light in gray, the "ra" sound lighting the word with an elegant glow. This has less to do with meaning as we commonly think of it and more to do with texture.

Although I once thought to title a book of poems *Gray Rhythms* before rejecting it as too literary, I doubt that even then I used *gray* in the senses described above. My chain of associations must be too personal to support Wallace Stevens' observation that "[a] new meaning is equivalent to a new word," but when I took on this assignment, *gray* was the first word that came to mind.

HALF-LIGHT | Maggie Hivnor

Would you know the meaning of the word, out of context? A spell-checker mistakes it for the half-life of some toxic element, but what it means is dusk, twilight, evening—as in the evening-out of day and night, perhaps. You must be outdoors or near a window to notice the changing light: the sun is setting, the air cools, birds gather in the treetops, clamoring to celebrate God knows what and then, gradually, go silent. The day is over.

I encountered the word once and only once in a line from a Yeats poem, "Of night and light and the half-light." The bumpy rhythm reminded me of a line my mother had described from Shakespeare's Sonnet 73: "When yellow leaves, or none, or few, do hang. . . ." She pointed out the pauses, the shifts of the eye, first to a view of golden foliage, then to the tree startlingly bare, and then back to a branch with just a few yellow leaves still clinging to it. That last branch catches the poet's gaze, so that you almost hold your breath, waiting to see if another leaf will drop off and flutter down. With a similar sweep of the camera, Yeats takes you in one line from night to light, and then back again to what is most striking, most fleeting: the half-light in between. "Had I the heavens' embroidered cloths, . . . The blue and the dim and the dark cloths / Of night and light and. . . ." With that one word, *half-light*, he provokes a vision of Irish gloaming and gentle intimacy.

Picture those "embroidered cloths" of heaven, "[E]nwrought with golden and silver light." Picture the green of the pasture deepening, while the clouds soften to some shade you've never seen before. If you live in the city, the streetlamps have been lit, the windows in the houses become small stage sets, and you can look in to see what paintings have been hung on other people's walls . . . but the sky is not yet dark; children are still playing in the park. If you are at the beach, the colors in the waves shift to rose, peach, salmon, reflecting the sky as she puts on more and more lascivious evening attire (lavender, gold, fuchsia), until she finally switches back to an elegant, blue-black silk. There is a long moment before one thing slips away, just as something new comes into focus, when they are there together, both changing and held suspended. Think of Steinhardt's late playing of Bach's Chaconne, Partita in D Minor, when he gives us, with one bow, watery trills of light and the somber current below. It feels as if it could go on forever.

Last summer, on a walk with my daughter, I mentioned again how much I love the time when lamplight vies with daylight. She told me her favorite word was *coruscate*, the verb form. *Coruscate?* I pictured glowing coals, but she said it means a sudden flash of light. Oh, sure, I thought, she would love that image; she can handle the glare. Half-light is for those of us further along, half-way on our journey—"Nel mezzo del cammin di nostra vita." When I want to see my husband's face in our darkened bedroom, I turn the shutters half open against the streetlamp's light sifting through the leaves, the headlights moving past, filtered into narrow bands: a quarter-light, a demisemiquaver-light, just enough.

Even if I had come across *half-light* many times since first reading Yeats, the patina that particular poem laid on the word would still gleam every time it came to mind. When poets use a word as well as that, they leave a trace of meaning on it, a fingerprint—or sheen: a new layer of lacquer, a warmth, like the time-worn glow on the newel post of an old banister, touched by generations. Intrigued by their shapes and textures, we gather up these words, just as any child would, or any paleontologist: *pandemonium* (Milton), *sing* (Homer), *freedom* (Martin Luther King, Jr.), *oyster* (Shakespeare), *tears* (Virgil). Imagine an infinity of pebbles on all the beaches, each stone bearing traces of its geological origins, and each then polished by different sands, different waves—while readers walk along the periphery, gathering specimens: *viscosity, linsey-woolsey, cellophane, scuppers, twit.* We all have our own private collections. We pass them on, adding our own layers of associations, to our friends and our children, just as we do family rituals or recipes. (Did the Irish write so well because they didn't have the right food to distract them? Was it because they couldn't woo their lovers with murgh makhani or goat cheese or olives that they resorted to rhyme? A quick history of the world might reveal an inverse relation between cultures with the most highly developed cuisines and those with the most moving lyrics. Have you ever tried garum, Roman fish sauce? What did the great poet Jalal al-Din Rumi have to eat in the Persian desert? What were William and Dorothy Wordsworth eating at Dove Cottage in the English Lake District in the 1800s: hard-boiled eggs, overcooked vegetables, mutton? What, for that matter, did Yeats have for supper—"a mess of shadows"?)

Half-light: you cannot say this without smiling, without opening your mouth, without touching your bottom lip with your teeth, and then using the tip of your tongue to sound the *l* and *t*. It's an airy word, enunciated in the front of the mouth. In

107

charades, you would have to break it up: two words, first word sounds like "laugh"; second word could be pantomimed as "not heavy"—or with a flashlight. Your teammates still might not get it, though. Who says *half-light* any more? This pebble is mostly out of circulation, off the beach.

"But I'm sure I've heard it before," my daughter says, "I think I've even used it in the phrase 'the half-light of morning.'" This sounds *all* wrong to me. The morning would be misty and damp, or glaring with sunrise; besides, in the morning one has too much work to do to notice the light changing. Half-light is about nightfall: fading, darkening and . . . loss. From college, she emails me her *half-light* sighting, in a song by the Decemberists: "The boys in denim vests . . . / Sweetly tipsy by the half-light / The light and the half-light." Ah, so these Decemberists have read Yeats and can spot a good word when they see one. Are they, too, young men already nostalgic for their own youth? I claim *half-light* as an older person's word (Yeats, aged at twenty-three)—not for rock bands: what do they know of the old, high courtesy? What do they know of the risk Yeats describes in "He wishes for the Cloths of Heaven"—his sense that we can never have enough to give those we love, or that in loving one has to offer everything, even dreams? What do they know of asking someone to "tread softly"? But then, I was my daughter's age when I first saw and loved the word. I first noticed it because of the meaning Yeats gives it in those lines, the feeling that there was someone he imagined thinking of lovingly and longingly day and night, night and day, but most especially at evening—*half-light*—when nature seems to pause, and the light cuts sideways across water, fields, or streets, so that trees stand next to their own shadows, reflecting on one day's passing and another's possibility.

HOPE | John Rodriguez

You will see your daughter every other weekend. You will need to call her mother to find out where your child will be. One day, you will be told to pick her up tomorrow at the train station like luggage.

Twelve subway cars, seven #5s and five #2s, will stop at Simpson Street between 3:55 and 4:35 and your daughter will not have been on any of them. You will leave a saucy message on your child's mother's answering machine, walk up Southern Boulevard to Izzy's, and buy a Fat Joe 560 long-sleeved T-shirt for $30, the second for $25, which means you're being jerked for at least five dollars but you're mad and want to represent your peoples.

There will be nothing on television or radio to take your mind off your daughter. You will call three more times, leaving one more message and hanging up as soon as the machine comes on twice. You will become desperate. You will call Roland. He's a court officer. A stranger will answer his cell phone. Fuck Roland. You will call Charley. The phone will ring until you almost find religion again. Her husband will say Mexican salutations, realize it's *un norte Americano* and put his wife, your oldest known crimey, ex-dope-fiend/stripper/prostitute-masseuse, multiple family and criminal court respondent and petitioner, on the phone. You will ask her about your options. Go to the precinct and say this woman left the state with your child, she says in between emasculating comparisons with members of her weak-willed cohort; you'll sign a report and they'll get you into her apartment. You will go to the precinct and fill out a report. A cop will say, we can't break down her door. You will ask, can I take the report to court. Sure, but we get fathers who come in here every weekend.

The idea of going to court, and waiting on line to be searched, and being searched, then metal-detected, combined with having been chumped by the cops, lectured by some scandalous female, and not seeing your daughter will make you feel like a very bad person. You will go to court the next afternoon so as not to wait with the criminal masses whom you are not a part of (really, you mean it) and be given a short form to fill out and return the next day at eight in the morning or four in the afternoon. Never having experienced night court, you will choose it.

You will arrive at 3:57. You will wait on line for twenty minutes to put down your form and wait. You will remember the army expression "Hurry up and wait." You will politely move your feet when bad-ass kids run past you again and again. There will be many bad-ass kids. There will be many people copping pleas on cell phones. There will be many people copping pleas out loud to no one in particular. All the men will curse. There will be many deadbeat dads. There will be many cuties whom you will not rap to because they will think you are a deadbeat dad. You will wonder if you are a deadbeat dad. You will not be called until 7:37. You will be given a court date two months in the future. Have someone, the beautiful woman filing your petition will say, at least eighteen give her the summons before eight days before the court date, not on a holiday or a Sunday or in a place of worship; I hope it works out. You will hope it works out.

H.O.T.T. | Rachel Toor

Beautiful, like *brilliant,* can be used only sparingly, in clean, well-lighted places, and never in reference to someone you actually know. Let's face it: no one, when you see them up close, is really beautiful or brilliant. They get zits, or make childish mistakes in grammar. They can have moments of beauty, or brilliance, and their work can be both beautiful and brilliant, but no one looks beautiful after two weeks of backwoods camping or when she has the flu.

Pretty is condescending. Little girls can be pretty, in pink or blue or polka dots. But not women. *Pretty* implies a kind of totality—that's all there is. Pretty women are never scary smart. On the other hand, girls can't be gorgeous. That's for grown-ups. As are the words that imply sex: *alluring, bewitching, enticing,* or *comely.* But who would use one of those words for someone with whom you've discussed NAFTA or the teleological suspension of the ethical?

Stunning, divine, elegant, dazzling all imply some kind of spectacle or evening wear. *Radiant* is for skin, *glowing* for pregnancy, and together they are usually used to describe the skin of those who are pregnant. *Lovely, exquisite,* and *classy* all reek of the patrician. *Shapely* means big-boobed; *statuesque,* basketball-player tall; and *Rubenesque,* of course, blubber-butt fat. *Handsome* implies horsey, as does *grand. Fine* used to be used as code for "attractive black woman." *Sexy* is icky, *foxy* snags like polyester pants, and *pulchritudinous* seems like it should mean the opposite of what it does. *Striking* is for someone who is clearly not pulchritudinous but whom you don't want to offend.

Cute gets a lot of work, particularly with regard to men who are too often too old, really, to be considered cute. Babies can be cute; puppies more so. *Attractive* and *good-looking* are all-purpose and vanilla. *Doable* is apt, though perhaps a bit rude.

During those horrid years of junior high and high school, my best friend, Lisan, was cute, pretty, and at times, when she wasn't camping or having the flu, even beautiful. She was tiny, with straight blond hair. Lisan was woman-shapely, with a nipped waist and hips that swelled to a figure skater's bottom. Her lips made a perfect bow, her skin was clear and often tanned, and her mother's hobby was shopping for clothes. Lisan was nonjudgmental, quick to make fun of herself, and frequently said things that only attractive women can get away with, like "I have to fart," or "I feel a poop coming on."

Lisan was my best friend at a time when it's important to have a best friend. We complained about our fathers; mine was icy and demanding, hers rheumy-eyed and distracted when he wasn't drinking. When he was, he was as frightening as mine. We took refuge in our own and each other's mothers. We logged hours lying on piles of quilts on the floor of her bedroom, followed each other into the bathroom so as not to interrupt conversations, and stayed up Saturday nights watching Gilda Radner wonder *Why all the talk about Soviet Jewelry?* We listened to Elton John and wore Huk-A-Poo shirts. She had multicolored toe socks. On her tiny feet they looked fantastic.

113

Around Lisan I could be the person I thought was me. With her I was confident and well-loved and supported. I also felt huge, hideous, unkempt, pimply, and poorly dressed, even when I was wearing her ivory Organically Grown sweater or seafoam Danskin leotard. I was skinny, and not in a good way. My legs were bowed, my skin pasty, and my pores large. My hair was never shiny; it waved and curved and, when it wasn't greasy, frizzed. My face was too long, my eyes were too close together, and don't even get me started on my teeth. I knew what one word best described my looks, but I never spoke it aloud. It is still the worst, harshest word I know: *ugly*. I was afraid to use it because I knew that someone would fling it back against me.

Lisan and I defined ourselves against the other. I was the more adept gymnast, mostly because I was fearless and competitive. She worked harder in school, but I got better grades. I was brazen when she was timid, wordy when she was reticent. She was the nice one, the girl who never argued with teachers. I was the kite, we would say to each other, and she the kite string. We appreciated this complementarity and I knew it was what made our friendship work. We talked about most of these differences. We were best friends, so we talked about everything. Except the one thing we didn't talk about: our looks.

❖

Having a pretty best friend was made worse by being the daughter of a beautiful woman. My mother's looks were the first thing people noticed about her. With auburn hair, long and wild—she was an artist—in miniskirts and high boots, my mother was a babe. Her wedding photos, she often told me, ended up in *Life* magazine. On nights when my parents were going out, I'd sit on the edge of the bathtub watching my mother spend hours kohling her eyes and rouging her cheeks.

She would leave behind a headache-inducing cloud of perfume. My mother cared a lot about her looks. About mine she never said a word.

I was smart. That was what counted. The message I heard—though contradicted by what I saw—was that outward appearance didn't matter. "That kind of thing is not important to us," was my parents' tag line about worldly possessions like good clothes, nice cars, or a fancy house. My father espoused the academic's jealous disdain of the bourgeoisie, though we did have an imported—and, in the 1970s, unusual—Peugeot car and lived in a large Victorian house with a grand piano my father insisted was a necessity.

My mother and I shared clothes, and she would sometimes offer that a blouse or skirt looked nice on me, but never that I myself looked nice, never that I was cute, or pretty, or even striking. As I grew up, she would notice when boys noticed me (*That guy was looking at you!*) but that was as far as it went. When I became an adult, she would comment on my appearance only retrospectively and comparatively: I like your hair better this way.

And so, in high school and later, I was surprised when boys found me attractive. I knew that I had a good body. When I wasn't standing next to Lisan, I was, officially, petite. I had slim, boyish hips and was, oddly, stacked. My ta-tas had sprouted, big and in Barbie-like disproportion to my small frame. In the late seventies and early eighties, my thick, long hair was easily blow-dried into a Farrah Fawcett mane. I almost grew into my two front teeth. I wasn't cute or pretty, but I was evidently, in some way, desirable, though it took the interest of a large number of young men to convince me of this.

I remember watching Ellen Barkin in the movie *The Big Easy* and searching for a word to describe her looks. She was not in any conventional way attractive; her face was nearly malformed.

Yet she was impossible not to look at. She had a killer body, and she sparked, exuded, heat. At the same time, her strange good looks never detracted from the sense that she was also intelligent and in complete control of her sexuality.

Over the years, I came to see myself as less ugly, and then, eventually, as not quite ugly at all. But I still didn't have a self-description that felt accurate. If pressed, when, say, authoring a personals ad, I could write that I was "reasonably attractive." That seemed about right. Over the years my body has changed only for the better. Middle-aged women tend to spread; marathon running has made me lean and muscular. Highlighting has kept me blond, and expensive products have made my hair periodically manageable. A little bit of money went a long way toward making my teeth something that I didn't have to cover when I smiled. A wealthy friend fits me in hand-me-down Prada and cashmere sweaters; she taught me that tighter looks better on me and doesn't lower my IQ.

❖

A handful of years ago I was dating a jaunty triathlete nearly a decade my junior. We'd gone to a party, where I'd met his best friend for the first time. I felt good and thought, unusually, that I looked good. My hair had cooperated that night and I was wearing the "ass pants"—beige, slightly stretchy trousers my rich friend's tiny daughter had recycled my way. They were fantastically posh, but more to the point, they fit me in such a way that complete strangers—always women—would say I had a great butt. I've come to believe that I have a perfectly fine—if not particularly shapely—caboose, but these pants do something magical to it.

In the car on the way home, my date was smirking. He was prone to smirking. I asked what was so amusing.

"It's what Dale said about you."

What, I wanted to know, had his best friend said?

"He said, 'Rachel's hot.'" He stretched out the word so that it sounded like haaaaa-ot.

"Rachel's haaaaa-ot," he said again.

Then he smiled full on, looked at me, and said, "Rachel is hot."

The next morning, still atwitter, I announced to my freshman comp students, apropos of nothing and probably inappropriately, that a guy had said I was hot. I had never before been called hot. I wasn't sure if I'd ever even used the word.

"You are hot," the girls said quickly. Then one added, "H.O.T.T.—hott!"

"Aitch Oh Tee Tee? Are you kidding me?"

They assured me this spelling implied really, really hot.

I spent the next few days trying out "Rachel's hot" the way you would a new pair of heels: after getting comfortable at home, I took it out on the streets. "Someone said I was hot," I'd tell a friend. "Well, you are," she would say. "Really?" My friends got annoyed with me. It's never fun to be asked to reassure someone. I reached the pinnacle of my hot-titude in the fall of 2004 at the age of forty-two. It was, mostly, a relief.

❖

Even if I may no longer be h.o.t.t., I am utterly smitten with a word that applies to everyone from *jolie-laide* Ellen Barkin to ethereal Uma Thurman to skanky Britney Spears. You can use it for men. Barack Obama, you have to agree, is hot. When I asked my friend Jeff to think of a woman whom he would refer to as hot, it took him about seven seconds to come up with Tina Fey. Tina Fey? I thought he was kidding. I mean, she's attractive, but would you really want to sleep with her? "Yes," he said, "Oh yes, I would. She's sooooo hot." I accused him of thinking she's hot just because she's so smart and funny and talented—and I proved my own point. He's right. Tina Fey is smokin' hot. But I didn't think that hers would be the first name on most men's list. So I asked the same question of my friend David, a massage therapist who came to his current job after a stint in Army Intelligence in Bosnia. Tina Fey? He wasn't with Jeff on that one. "No, if you want to know who's hot," he said, "it's Janeane Garofalo."

This is why I love my male friends. And it's why I love the word *h.o.t.t.* It's not about straight white teeth, heart-shaped bottoms, and good hair. It's all about the important things that make us attractive. If it had been around when I was younger, applicable to people instead of just cars, I would—I truly believe this—have had a different life. I could have turned out to be an entirely different person. Better. Less edgy. More confident and gregarious. If I had been called hot when I was a teenager, I might really be Aitch Oh Tee Tee H.O.T.T.

_I_ | Cynthia Gaver

_I_: the ninth letter and, nine being, numerologically, the number representing endings, the symbol of such.

The only constantly capitalized pronoun of the English alphabet. Subjective, it often comes at the beginning of a sentence and impels some action, such as "I make money" or "I'll buy it," "I'm hungry," "I'll eat anything," or "I can pay in cash or credit"; also useful for inducing (or inveighing) others toward the ends of one's individual desires, such as "I want you to make this happen," or "I'll need you to ____," or "I would like it very much if you would do____ for me," _me_ being the objective but equally useful pronoun counterpart to the actor "I."

The ambitious and fast-sailing prodigy of its distant ancestor _ego_, having tossed the jetsam of two extra letters and raised its mast capital-high. Though the Spanish _Yo_, the French _Je_, the Chinese _Wo_, the Arabic _Ana_, and the Russian _Ya_, for instance, are sleek, expedient, and perhaps more melodic, the English equivalent capitalizes on brevity and efficiency and introduces the first-person singular, the most important point of view in its indigenous lingual culture.

The instigating beginning to such therapy-session fillers as "I think," "I feel," and "I'm confused," "I'm experiencing," and "I'm re-evaluating"; to such legal document standards as "I hereby," "I attest," "I have read," "I agree to," and "I bequeath"; and to such inane conversational noise as "I'm Mandy, Mark, Minnie, Mahatma, Morrie, Mork," and so on to the second level of social-conversational noise with the insipid and obligatory "I'm fine," to the more digestible, "I'm good," to the nauseating "I'm terrific!" Also useful at the third level of social interaction and interrogation—"What do you do?"—and the response which determines the length, breadth, and interest in further conversation: "I'm an engineer," "I'm an internist," "I'm a legal assistant," "I'm an illegal immigrant," "I'm a student," "I'm the town idiot," "I'm an insurance claims adjustor," or the ever-popular "I'm actually between jobs right now," to the refreshingly honest "I'm an indigent, indispensable, and unemployed intellectual," to the never-popular "I'm independently wealthy. I live off my investments."

The homonym of *e-y-e*, the "organ of sight for vertebrates" (*Random House Webster's*, 1999) and the reported "mirror of" or "window to" the soul.

The letter often confused visually with the number one. For the impenitent upwardly-mobile and the irretrievably self-absorbed (these categories collapse and overlap significantly) there is no confusion.

The vowel, letter, word, pronoun found in 612,000,000 Google hits. (Interestingly enough, the number-one hit was Disney.com.)

Doubled, bridged at its vertical midpoint, and given an *e*, it becomes the second most important subjective-case pronoun, *he.* Adjoin the serpentine *s* to this (a tribute, perhaps, to Eve and her invertebrate friend) and you have the less powerful subjective-case pronoun *she.*

The one almost insignificant exception to a universe of "other."

The loneliest vowel/letter/word and associative number "that you'll ever do."

The constant.

ICKYBICKY | Megan Kossiakoff

Term used to describe an exploded ballpoint pen as it is carefully being extracted from the bottom of a backpack.

INTERESTING | Jayson Iwen

I've been keeping an eye on this word for years now, conducting a stake-out in a van across the street from where it lives. I hate the word in writing, yet savor it in speech. In writing it's merely a placeholder for better words, while in speech it's damning praise of a sublime order. *Interesting* is its own antonym, its own shadowy other.

But that's not exactly why I'm watching it. That's not why I'm wary of uttering the word. I'm suspicious of the root that feeds it. *Interesting* entered common usage in the century that birthed modern capitalism. In its first appearance in print the word was explicitly linked to that economic context: ". . . that Passion which is esteem'd peculiarly interesting; as having for its Aim the Possession of Wealth" (Shaftesbury, 1711). Not surprisingly, viewed from this new old angle, contemporary definitions of the word leap to attention and assume the stance of marketing terminology: "adapted to excite interest; having the qualities which rouse curiosity, engage attention, or appeal to the emotions" (*OED*). In short, since detecting capitalist ideology in this most unassuming and pervasive of words, I've begun to worry it's inside every word, though its outline may only be visible in those that poorly conceal it, like sheets draped over ill intents.

Do I expect something "interesting" to gain in value over time, to somehow return my attention with interest? Do I find myself using this word because, consciously or not, though I know I cannot know the future, I know that seemingly insignificant things might, someday, be priceless? Do I therefore call all such suspects interesting? Another dated usage of the word seems, at first, unrelated to its current usage, unless we think of something "interesting" as something which grows and accumulates value over time. An "interesting condition, situation, or state" was, not long ago, a euphemism for pregnancy, while an "interesting event" was, likewise, a euphemism for birth. Something passional becoming something economic. This is the kind of unconscious logic I'm afraid might be firing through dark channels of my brain whenever I speak.

I fear this because many days I feel finite. I feel spendable. I see my window into existence shrinking and the objects of my attention looming in that diminishing frame. They're either becoming my world or they're blocking my view of it. They add value to my life or they rub my face in my own inevitable end. I realize, however, that this is not a truth. It's belief. And, though belief is both stronger and more dangerous than truth, it is, thankfully, alterable.

Of the moment of death, Marcus Aurelius said, "Our loss is limited to that one fleeting instant, since no one can lose what is already past, nor yet what is still to come—for how can one be deprived of what one does not possess?" "But, Mr. Aurelius," a student of capitalism might counter, "consider how, through corporations and estates, one's possessions might live on after one's death, in the tangible spirit of legal entities, how one may continue to lay claim to precious resources long after death.

Can we not possess the future by shrewd planning? Can we not attain all our desires through the investment of enough labor? Surely a child's death is more tragic than an adult's, because the child loses possession of greater time." Though we may be subject to some intoxicating beliefs, I think we still know how Aurelius would answer his own rhetorical question. Probably with another question. Something like, "How can you live now, if your mind is elsewhere?"

When I say *interesting* now, I ask myself, "Exactly what is it you think will repay you with interest?" And the answer is usually as inevitable as it is startling. So I sit here, drumming my fingers on the steering wheel, waiting for it to appear. Because it would feel so good to put it away forever. Go ahead, I say to myself. Say it.

INVISIBLE | Dan Machlin

"What was invisible to you?"

"Her hair, her lips, everything."

"And what about her voice?"

"I wouldn't say *invisible*. Maybe insubstantial. I would say lost. Lost to the room. Lost to the air. Able to be perceived, but only in the negative of its resonance."

"As if there were no *her* in her?"

"Yes, and only then could I recall her."

Rarely do you come across a word with such inherent nostalgia—a word with untold mystery and magic. *Invisible* is a traveler. It harkens us back, with its shimmering meaning, to the different eras of its use. It carries the weight of intellectual longing—Plato's invisible world of forms outside the cave of our sensual existence. And it recounts the origins of visibility itself: the Gnostic Apocryphon of John, which tells of the incomprehensible spirit who preceded the material universe, who was somehow visible to himself in his surrounding light, but invisible to all others.

There is also the eighteenth-century philosopher Salomon Maimon's humorous recounting in his autobiography of his attempt to learn practical (some would say magical) Kabbalah from his teacher, and with it *roeh veeno nireh* (the ability to see but make oneself invisible to others). After diligently following his teacher's instructions with hopes of using the ability for all the wrong reasons, he makes a fool of himself by believing he has succeeded.

Invisible bears us into the future, in an age where the virtual seems to render our traditional notions of visibility obsolete. Yet, it is the virtual that makes Thoreauvian retreat from the world (longing for invisibility) increasingly difficult. And it is the virtual, like an invisible aether, that instantly disseminates invisible security threats, from which we must be protected in equally invisible (and nefarious) ways.

The literary and filmic legacy of *invisible* can't help but offer stiff warning to any who dare attempt to employ it in their writing. There is H. G. Wells' tale of fallen morality, *The Invisible Man*, and its long string of B-movie and TV incarnations that haunt our collective memory. There is the brilliant doubling of Wells' title by Ralph Ellison in his allegory of race and social invisibility, *Invisible Man*, echoed by the constancy of the word's sociopolitical contemporary use: "the invisible poor," "invisible workers," "invisible children." Finally, there is Calvino's *Invisible Cities*, which depicts an empire and history that exists only by virtue of its telling.

But it is the sound qualities of this word that siren me back "in," just when I am prepared to walk away from such a meaning-laden linguistic enterprise. Consider the pure alliterative journey of *invisible*: vowel sounds that sweep you through, catch you with staccato syllables pivoting around the *s* at the center, then suddenly release you forward.

Invisible pulls the wool over our eyes by employing a prefix that is both preposition and negation. And *invisible* also reminds us of *inscape*, Gerard Manley Hopkins' term to describe the complex of characteristics which embody every unique thing in the world.

But perhaps what I relish most about the word *invisible* is the way in which it underscores the relativity and arbitrariness of perception. It promises either a devilish act of concealment or, much more profoundly, a failure of that original Gnostic light—of the self's ability to place itself in the world.

KANKEDORT | Maureen N. McLane

> *Was Troilus nought in a kankedort?*
> —Chaucer, *Troilus and Criseyde*, II. 1752

Isolate, peculiar, rare, obsolete, it surfaces in the language only once, according to the latest edition of the *Oxford English Dictionary*: in Chaucer's *Troilus and Criseyde*. *Kankedort*: speculatively defined as a "difficult situation" by Larry B. Benson, editor of *The Riverside Chaucer* (OUP, 1987); further glossed in the *OED* as "a state of suspense; a critical position; an awkward affair."

A lonely word whose definition can only be inferred from its single, immediate context in Chaucer's poem: Troilus awaits his beloved, Criseyde, who is being led by her uncle Pandarus to Troilus's room for their first love-meeting. Pandarus—who throughout the poem behaves like unto his name, serving as pander, go-between, near-pimp of Criseyde. Here at the very end of Book II the lovesick Troilus awaits his long-sought love, and nervously considers how to declare his passion:

> *And was the firste tyme he shulde hir preye*
> *Of love; O mighty God, what shal he seye?*
> (II. 1756–7)

Was Troilus nought in a kankedort? Was he not at a difficult, critical moment, that abyssal moment before erotic disclosure? Was he not worrying about the right words to say, the right words to elicit the right response, the lover's answering love, the body perhaps then pledged, then possessed? It's only humans, as far as we know, who can use words to get bodies together. The word as the body evanesced in a breath, a breath bearing intelligible sound. *What shal he seye?* What does he say?

> *Lo, the alderfirste word that hym asterte*
> *Was, twyes, "mercy, mercy, swete herte!"*
> (III. 97–8)

"Language is fossil poetry," Emerson declared in his essay "The Poet" (1844); some poetry becomes the amber in which the delicate fossils of a language are embedded. *Was Troilus nought in a kankedort?*

"A dream of a common language," Adrienne Rich imagined, a difficult dream. *Kankedort* falls out of this dream. Words grow obsolete, languages die, texts become the tombs of the dead only some learn to reanimate. *Kankedort*: a *hapax legomenon*, to invoke a technical term of the Greek grammarians, themselves interested especially in those words that appeared only once in the Homeric corpus. *Kankedort* a *hapax* in Chaucer's *Troilus and Criseyde* but also in the English language itself. The *OED* marks *kankedort* as not only rare but obsolete.

You find yourself in a "difficult situation."

You're asked to choose a word that has meant something to you, an invitation that lends itself to thoughts of the exceptional word, the unusual word, of a word that lodged itself like a mystery,

a word that gathered around it associations so personal and rami-
fying that the word itself becomes the sign of an epoch not only
in Troilus's life but in your own. There are words the dictionary
deems "rare," "obsolete," "slang," "obscene": lexicographers can
debate such classifications and have. There are words that are
"rare" for the general and words that are "rare" for you, words
that are "obsolete" in the language and those that are "obsolete"
for you: *Christian; fuckwad; wife.* That your mind runs this way,
running aground on the reef of *kankedort,* of *dulcarnoun* (*Troilus
and Criseyde* III. 931), of *spatchcocked, onomoastics,* and other such
shoals, shows your tendency toward verbal fetishism, or more precisely, lexical fetishism: one could ponder the depths of the com-
monest words—*thing,* or *think* (as Wordsworth does, incessantly);
love, kind (see Shakespeare); the overwhelming power encoded
in the humblest parts of speech, prepositions or articles, through
which every basic relation shines forth. *On. With. Together. Toward.
Between. The the* (Wallace Stevens).

To focus on the word is to focus on "a part of speech," yet no
one I know ever spontaneously spoke the word *kankedort.* Perhaps only Chaucer himself ever spoke the word *kankedort.* He was
charting his way through one of the four major dialects then jos-
tling for the privilege of ascending into a more standard "Englysshe": Chaucer's "Englysshe" will beat out John Gower's, and
that of the *Ancrene Wisse,* and other thirteenth-century variants
then available on the island of Britain. If you concentrate, you
can almost read Chaucer without a gloss, even if contemporary
English—whatever that might be—is your only language.

What shal he seye?

What should I say of *kankedort* other than the word
constellates a time, a time of reading, a time of slow dawning
and changing, of delicate then desperate realizing over many
months and belatedly that I was in a kankedort; I was sick with
love; I was in love with another; I knew not what to do; I did

almost nothing; I found myself at dulcarnoun, at my wittes ende; I almost did something bold; I didn't; then I did; then the plot changed, or its true drift was revealed—if only in retrospect.

> *Myn owen swete herte.*
> *Kankedort.*

The harsh Teutonic consonants surfacing amidst Chaucer's romance syllables, his rhyme words more typically the elegant courtly polysyllables of a Norman French: *mischaunce; purveaunce; dalliance. Kankedort* seems to leave romance languages behind, calling up that other register of an emergent English, drawing upon Anglo-Saxon and other Germanic wells. It is striking that when Criseyde finds herself later at wit's end, in a dilemma, she invokes a technical term from medieval Latin itself derived from Arabiç: *I am . . . at dulcarnoun,* she declares—invoking a term that seems to arise from a crux in geometry. It was always mixing, appropriating, bedeviling, this Englysshe.

The woman with whom I read *Troilus and Criseyde* and through whom I discovered *kankedort* died recently; she is beyond worldly care; I could hope that she, like Troilus,

> *ful blissfully is went*
> *Up to the holughnesse of the eighthe spere*
> (V. 1808–9)

but such metaphysics would falsify what I took to be her enthusiastic embrace of this single palpable world. After his death Troilus is *stellified*—that is, he is turned into a star, circling in the heavens, now stoic, now amazed to ponder human folly:

> *And in hymself he lough right at the wo*
> *Of hem that wepten for his deth so faste.*
> (V. 1821–2)

Before she died she told a friend she planned to return as an owl. I can imagine her like Troilus surveying *this litel spot of erthe*, though she unlike Troilus would be more willing to perch on merely earthly branches.

LASAI | Elizabeth Macklin

Lasai (pronounced la-sigh, accent on either syllable, depending): In Basque, *lasai* is an adjective or adverb and, as the root form of a verb, can be a command, or even an invocation, and in my opinion is onomatopoetic. Or—more than that—is an onomatopoeia squared, since not only does it say its own name but also, if you repeat it a few times slowly (or even just a little more slowly), you become it.

Dictionary definitions include "calm," "tranquil," "carefree," "untroubled." (And "relaxed," "loose," for clothing and also behavior. *Lasaiegi hezitako haurrak* means "Children who were raised too lasai.") None of the English words or expressions for calming down, no matter how deeply attractive they may be, work in the same way *lasai* does; in fact, it sometimes seems that every English command for calming down all too quickly accrues impatience.

In Spanish *lasai* is *tranquila*—a gain of two hard consonants and the roll of an *r*. (What men say to a woman for "Take it easy" in Spanish is *Tu tranquila*—the very phonemes sound irritable to me. Women to women usually just say *Tranqui-i-i-i-la*, drawing

134

out the lulling part.) And since in Spain's Basque Country the word *tranquila* has bled across languages, in Basque-speaking circles it is often possible to tell when someone is getting impatient by noting whether what has come out is *lasai* or *tranki*.

I'm told over the border on the Basque Country's French side people have, in the last decade or so, been using a new expression to supplement *lasai*: *zen*. The word *zen* has always existed in Basque, but as a verb, meaning "he/she/it was." (No gender in the third person.) But now Basque-speaking people in Bayonne or Ciboure or Pau might say, holding out a soothing hand, palm downward, "Zen." I haven't determined whether, just inside the Buddhist, conceptual spin, they ever hear an echo of the "was" in there.

The Basque language works by aggregation, and *lasai* turns up in a string of compound words. *Lasaikeria* (-*keria* being the suffix for "excess") is "wantonness," "abandon." A *lasaialdia* (-*aldi* being "a time for") is a time-out—useful for parents to have something constructive to suggest as the time-out begins. (If baseball were close-captioned in Basque, "Lasai" would have flashed onscreen repeatedly toward the end of a tight game on a damp night at Shea, as first baseman Keith Hernandez knelt to scrape the mud out of saver Sid Fernandez's cleats, and talk him down.) If the deep-breathing function of *lasai* should ever fail to work, a *lasaigarria*—"cause," "origin"—is a tranquilizer, or sedative.

LILAC | Joan Connor

The word has about it the scent of its referent, the light liquids sliding to that conclusive consonant. Its etymology matches its color, and one of its meanings is its color—that indigo, pale purple tint.

In *The Language of Flowers* lilac means innocent love. My first kiss blossomed in a lilac bush, crushed into a boy named Jack amid those grapey clusters of tiny star flowers, brushed by heart-shaped leaves. That delicate scent now miscible in memory with first kisses.

Like most things delicate, the lilac passes quickly when the weather turns warm; the tiny blossoms brown and drop, the scent no longer billowing through the house. That conclusive *c*. I associate them with New England springs, the tentativeness of beginnings, windows thrown open wide to the fullness of hope. As in the Whitman poem, New Englanders tend to plant them in the dooryards.

LILAC ONE:

When I was a girl, my family had a lilac bush, an accomplished one, an industrious one, a historical one, outside our

136

first home in Maine, likely as old as the yellow farmhouse it ornamented. We moved from that house in the early sixties and I did not return to it until two summers ago with my father.

I had returned to the house and town, blueprinted in memory, many times in my imagination, longing for springs on the Mousam River at ice-out, the rush of water over the dam, the cool blue days with scumbled clouds, the sudden green.

The occasion of our return was sad. We were headed to a lake where my aunt, my mother's last remaining sister, had drowned. We were picking up my badly shaken mother. En route we passed through our old town, Springvale. I did not recognize it as the setting of my memory and of many stories written in the intervening years: gone, the old tenement house; gone, the old row house; gone, the old woolen mill; gone, Uncle Billy's, where a crusty, noncommittal coot doled out woeful lobsters; gone, the soda fountain; gone, the old candy store with the curved glass cases with mummified stock from the thirties—coconut bacon strips, orange circus peanuts, licorice wax mustaches, candy dots on paper. (Nonetheless we ate them.) In their stead—condos, coffee shops, chichi dress shops, real estate agencies, and financial advisors. A water view is a water view.

We rolled up to our old house, and, while better kept, it looked much the same—attached barn with a mow, wrap-around porch, shuttered windows—although picketed now by a fence. Dad and I got out of the car and peeked over the fence. The meadow still sloped to the river, and the lilac still throve.

Back in the car, Dad remarked how sad he was about how much the town had changed.

I agreed; I preferred my memory of it. But I also felt a revenant relief. Since moving to Ohio, I had been homesick for New England. Seeing the town marked the end of yearning; it no longer existed. That conclusive *c.*

We drove on in silence to retrieve my mother.

LILAC TWO:

My husband and I lived in Old Town Alexandria in Virginia, but we also had a summer cottage on Chebeague Island, Maine, in Casco Bay. In the spring, I scrambled to return to the island by the end of May before the lilacs browned. The lilac bush adorned the corner—no doubt a former dooryard—of a cellar hole that tumbled in front of our cottage just across our clamshell driveway. It was not our bush but its perfume was, windows and screen doors open to the offshore breeze which mixed its scent with salt, redfish, clam flats.

I spent fourteen summers on the island renovating our small shingled cottage. I knew it floorboard by floorboard, winter ice jam leak by winter ice jam leak, leaky washer by leaky washer. I painted, laid tile, jacked up porches, glazed windows, spackled, sheetrocked, plumbed, shuttered, wired, papered walls, upholstered, snaked lines, gardened, mowed, and cut down trees. Then we divorced.

I often walk through the house down the mazy corridors of dreams. Knowing it so well, I never entirely left it.

Last year my son told me his father had put the cottage on the market.

During the winter, I was in Freeport, Maine, to teach. I decided to use my day off to ferry over and take a last peek in the winter windows. Fewer people are on-island in the cold months so I could count on being a summer-girl uninterrupted.

Once on the island I began the short walk to my former home, noting the changes—the store gone from the stone pier, the new ostentatious houses clamoring between the quieter clapboard and shingled homes I remembered. The sea air blasted my face. No snow but as cold as a witch's tit, the old New Englandism. I turned right onto North Road and wrapped my coat more tightly against the savage wind. No one walked the road. No car passed. A smart person knows when to stay put. I gained our small clamshell driveway, *ours* no longer. The pine trees Ed Duff, a previous tenant, had planted, one for each of his granddaughters, had grown stalky and sparse and no longer obscured the house from the road. Otherwise, the cottage looked much as it had, a little more neglected—peely paint, holey screens. I tipped forward toward the sills, window by window, to peer into the rooms—my son's nursery, the cheery red kitchen with its white wainscoting and salvaged antique glass cabinet I hung with my brother, the bath, the living room with its captain's desk, the dining room with its built-in china cabinet and hanging brass Heritage lantern—and what startled me, chilling me more than the fierce wind, was that nothing had changed. I stared into time arrested. Armchairs in their places. Gimbaled candleholder on the wall. The tide clock. The hutch in the dining room I had assembled. The details, down to the cushions I had embroidered with chickenscratch, gingham curtains, and braided rugs, remained the same. I left the house for the last time fifteen years ago, one year longer than my husband and I had been together. He rented it out since we had separated. But it remained the same. I felt as if I were staring into a former version of myself, haunting my own life. Vicarious. Voyeuristic. Split? Twinned? Parallel?

I squinted through the front door window up the stairs. I could not enter, but I did know this. If you entered, climbed the stairs, and turned right, the guest bedroom there was painted Wedgwood blue, the closets were calico-curtained, and in the back of the second closet behind some foul-weather gear, my wedding dress dangled, dimity cotton with a lace-up front, a lonely little ghost. People on an island rarely part with anything.

Behind me, the leafless branches of the lilac bush clattered their conclusive *c*'s. I understood their message; this was a summer house, and it was no longer mine. As I walked down the clamshell driveway, I noticed the For Sale sign, blown over into the ditch.

LILAC THREE:

When I moved with my son to Ohio, I bought a house unlike any I had lived in previously. I have always preferred old houses with their quirks and crannies and crazy angles, their sense of history and the people who have come before me, the hand-hewn beams and draw-planed wood, the wide board floors glowing with the patina of age, the bubbled glass, the unpredictability of them.

Instead I bought a vinyl-sided, wall-to-wall carpeted, prefab mock colonial that cut every corner just this side of the building code. At least it had two stories, which my son had insisted on. If I was to raise him alone far from friends and family and start a new career, then I needed a home that was at least efficient, ideally in need of little work and maintenance, and in a safe neighborhood crawling with kids. Ours was suburban, all the more peculiar to me as nowhere was there an urb to be seen. Urbs either.

Perhaps to make myself feel better, I planted a lilac bush in the backyard by the corner of our deck. But the soil here is clay, the climate far more humid and far hotter than in the Northeast. Frequently the leaves silver with fungus, then brown and rattle after May. The bush blossoms during odd seasons, sometimes fall, sometimes winter, this spring not at all. When it does bloom, I snip a few branches and place them in a vase beside my bed to waft me into sleep. They quickly turn and drop their small dried flowers onto my table. But for a few nights, I am home again.

In cooler New England the bushes can remain in bloom for a month. Here they can go by in two days. The lilac is New Hampshire's state flower.

My son now lives in the Northeast. I have lived here in Ohio far longer than I ever anticipated or desired, thirteen years.

The lilac, like me, struggles but is still here. We wait together for that conclusive *c.*

Last night I dreamed I heard children on the other side of the bush, some mischievous susurrus. I could not hear them clearly but suspected they were up to some boyish malice. "What do you want here?" I called in the dream.

Then two small pale hands parted the lilac branches scooping a bird's nest into the nest of their palms. "Just this."

Just this woven bowl of grass nestled in a November lilac.

Lilac, the echolalic *l*'s, the short murmur to that hard *c.* The lilting music dropping, stopping in the key of that hard *c.*

LINE | Eleanor Wilner

I am wondering about this request to say something about "a word." As a person of many words, I find the singular form of that noun somewhat daunting as a subject for thought. A word by itself seems to me like the proverbial lost ball in tall weeds. Where to begin looking? A proper noun, like the name of a city on a station sign, or a ball player's name on the back of his shirt, seems like cheating, since to name a place or a person is to have a world open from it automatically, like an unfolding fan.

A word in isolation: perhaps a foreign word, which has a singular identity in an English line, and its very strangeness is its seduction, but also its risk; for instance, *shantih*, which, in a poem of hers, Sujata Bhatt chided T. S. Eliot for using as he did with such solemnity, since, she wrote, it was an everyday word in India, one her mother used when she wanted the children to quiet down. Then, too, giving prominence to a single word invites magnification, makes the shadow of the looming Capital Letter darken the scene, arousing fear of The Word—of which in the Beginning there was supposedly but One, and from which notion follow a thousand exclusions and the sanction of countless crimes.

142

So, how to circumvent this army of objections, this resistance that rises in me from a nevertheless intriguing request? What word, what improper noun, like Walt Whitman, could contain multitudes? And that is when I think of a word that recurs, in poem after poem, like a perennial in a garden, but is, by both definition and connotation, so protean that it never seems to be the same thing twice and yet, changeable as it is, is connective in its essential nature, requiring, in its most abstract and mathematical definition, more than one point, and frequently a multiplicity of them.

The word is *line*, which, yes, is also, obviously, the unit of verse prosody; and *that*, however obvious, is one of the points, giving the word a kind of punning reflexiveness back to the linguistic action in which it is used, and to which meaning is inextricably bound. *Line* is one of those words whose complex nature poetry requires: that is, it has abstract meaning *and* concrete presence, so that it can (*pace* Archibald MacLeish) both mean *and* be. And both its concrete and abstract meanings are multiple and variable with context; when the world in which the word takes shape alters, so does the meaning.

Years ago a British editor objected to my repeated use of a rather blatant enjambment, calling the words "elbows" that were broken off from their syntactic units and sticking out at the end of a line. (*Get your elbows off the table*, a voice echoes from childhood.) At the time, partly to deflect criticism (I was young and in those days it still stung), and partly for the sheer pleasure of talking back to such a man in a language I associated with English literature and the traditional "feminine arts," I made, inadvertently, what amounted to a discovery (which is to say, before I insisted on defending what I have since decided was a failure of craft, I hadn't seen how supple, substantial, and curvilinear the poetic line was for me). I answered him, affecting the voice of a nineteenth-century woman that, my dear sir,

143

before I had picked up the pen, I had worked with needle and thread, and thus think of the line not as a unit or bar of type in a gridlike series, but rather as a thread, a flowing, sinuous and continuous thread of connection—the end of a line resembling a bend in a river, the noticeable break in syntax meant to mime that flow around the bend, from there to the next line in the poem.

Kidding or not, it seemed that I had articulated a formal intention of which I'd been unaware. Indeed, checking with the *OED*, I discover that the etymology of the word was the very material I had invoked: *line* coming from the same root as *linen*, both coming from the Latin, *linea*: "linen thread," beneath which was the root *linum*, or "flax," from which thread is spun. And I was, in fact, in the poetic business of turning a grid line into a thread, and that thread, which had been, like the nineteenth-century woman I invoked, part of a condition and a design into which so many of us had been bound as surely as a figure is sewn into a tapestry—a line which I was anxious to cut, free the bound subject from the elegant, tight design, and turn that line, in a manner of speaking, and (as my metaphor of the river bend had already announced) into a stream: syntax a connective, open-ended flow, medium and message an inseparable pair, and, if I may play one more change on the word: a lifeline.

MIDNIGHT | Willett Thomas

We're sitting alone in near dark, just me and my stepbrother. I am seven; he is nine. We are in a blue midnight kind of dark, the sort we will only remember, when adults, as a vague velvet backdrop for a thousand summer vacations to come and go before our parents' divorce.

Our stoop of choice is Miss Lydie's. We are bored neighbor children from the city, content for the moment to listen in the night to the opening and closing of kitchen cabinets bringing forth the clank and clink of dishes placed on Formica counters, green and yellow, some with swirls, some with the patterns all but gone, followed not too distantly by the crunch of sea fossils from a million years gone by as the family man's Buick pulls into the driveway, a bit of dirt run made by brothers' cars, uncles' cars, neighbors' cars, all the very same model the salesman Mr. Pete/Mr. Pete, Jr., says was designed especially for "folks like us," with the sound it makes, the scrape of metal on metal as the driver's side door opens, then closes, to announce the arrival of the man in the panama hat. Maybe it's Mr. James this time, home from the insurance office, or, perhaps, Mr. Tuttle, home early

from his dry-cleaning store. "Hey, Mister James—Mister Tuttle."
"Hey, you there, yourself. What you know good?" Ending with
the slam of the Buick's back door or trunk, signaling that there
are groceries to be unloaded, more likely than not, something
needed for that night's supper, not a nerve pill or two for
your mama, found in a little white pharmacy bag in the glove
compartment. No, this is produce, green and leafy, shooting
out from the tops of brown paper sacks, or maybe bread rolls,
wedged against the greens, or perhaps the meat itself, near the
bottom, along with a goodie to be found later, deep inside the
man's breast pocket, but that's only if your daddy is the sort
to be found wearing a panama hat, the kind with the black
band or the ultimate smooth-talker, gent's style, with a feather
sticking out to the side, but clearly at a slant. No, more likely,
your daddy, not unlike our own, is one of the ones to be found
wearing a baseball cap cocked to the side or a bandana pushed
back off his head, one of those tired and sweaty men shuffling
home from the wharf in the dark, shouting, cursing, calling
to his kid in the distance, "Where you at, boy?," his summons
barely heard over late-breaking waves . . . hidden within the
blue midnight, now that it is truly no longer day, but night one
more time.

NEGLIGEE | Jane Delury

At nine PM in a world capital you can buy carelessness. On the floor of the changing room, my sweater and pants and underwear, my bra and socks with the heels worn sheer. From the spread of ceiling, halogen bulbs, half-hooded like the eyes of a lizard, beam down benevolent light to better obscure the mirror's reflection. This was not the white light of the doctor's office, not the unforgiving light of noon that unmasks the skin. This was false light, teasing light, the light of a bedside lamp, from a closet door opened just a crack.

Negligee. Not this word, stripped of its accents and adorned with an unnecessary *e*, but the word it really is, *négligé*— neglected, slapdash—which, as I write this, my computer tries to bring into line, forcing the extra *e*, piping the true word red. A woman, propped against pillows, waits for the water to stop its run through the pipes in the wall. Behind the translucent curtain of silk hedged with stiff ruffle, her diaphragm sucks in her belly. Her legs splay with studied indifference over the bed.

147

This tatter of storm cloud that scuds over panties snapped at the crotch, this spider-web garment that fits in a pocket, is the great-great-granddaughter of the bedroom gowns worn by the women of the eighteenth-century French court. High on the throat, grazing the navicular bones of the feet. The obverse reflection of the dresses born about during the day, nothing of transparence or divulgence to these loose yards of linen. But for this: without the armature of corsets and panniers, her body moves unbound. *Je suis en négligé*, I'm not dressed, she would say to the knock at the door. Then sit on the edge of her bed or look out the window, freed from the leaden skirts, the complication of petticoats, her body like the Montgolfier balloon just risen over the skyline of Paris, its nonchalant drifting an illusion as two men stand by ready to force the descent. She can feel the spread of her body, but unlike the woman listening to the water, she delights in the way the fat slips into the crevices of the skin, the way her uncaged lungs take in the air of her room.

In the bar of my hotel, alone in this city, I wound the silver watch traded for the negligees given to me by distant cousins before my wedding. One of them sat in a corner and twisted the ribbons from the packages into a pastel anemone, which I later discarded. *Negligee.* How the word rises to the roof of the mouth. I asked where I could find one, then walked out the lobby into the night. Above my head, through the gold-trimmed ceiling, on hundred-count sheets, lay women in negligees. Women who, downstairs at the bar, opened their mouths around their wine glasses so that their lipstick would not leave a stain.

How did *negligee* lose its negligence, submit to the scissors of meaning? On that cover of *Life* magazine, Rita Hayworth tips toward the wall, her breasts crystallized by black lace, the skin of her shoulders woven and fitted to the sweep of her bones. In the changing room, you could not see the shimmer of stretch marks at my waist, the belly my husband cups in his hand when we fall asleep, stretched out by my daughters who, in ten years or so, will come to stores like this one to buy the babydolls, the thongs. I thought I could not believe in the theatrics of it, but I believed her, that woman in the mirror, who looked back at me.

NUT | Andrew Hudgins

nut, *n.*

1. The hard-shelled fruit of certain trees, such as a pecan, walnut, hazelnut, or almond.
2. Slang (usually plural, *nuts*): Testes.
3. Slang: A crazy person. Plural: *nuts,* the state of being crazy.

My uncle's fastball hit the grass just behind the green pine cone that was home plate, bounced just beneath the fingertips of my glove, and, leaping upward, whammed into my scrotum. I jammed both hands down the front of my shorts, clutched my crotch, fell over the grass, and curled around my testicles, which felt like they suddenly constituted seventy percent of my body mass. A *throbbing, inflamed* seventy percent.

"Once he gets a few breaths in him, he'll be okay," my uncle, standing over me, informed my brothers and the neighbor kids who'd gathered around to observe my suffering. "He's just been hit in the nuts."

"Nuts!" I thought, my hands cupped around them. "I've never heard them called *that* before."

In my house the things that hung below the thing we called my "thang" were *testicles.* It was a word we made a point not to have frequent need of. At school they were *balls,* which troubled me because balls were perfectly round and my testicles were not. And though I assumed that other boys' were not round either, I had not, at ten, initiated an inquiry on the subject.

Lying on the ground at the base of a neighbor's azalea, crying in pain, gasping for breath, I cupped my nuts and thought, "That's it! He's right. They're nuts!" But after this spasm of illumination, I kept thinking. They weren't exactly like nuts—just more like nuts than they were like balls. Though slightly oblong, they weren't elongated, like pecans. Walnuts were closer in shape, but larger than what I was holding. Hazelnuts, lopsided but nearly spherical, were an even better match in shape, but not in size. The teardrop shape of almonds removed them from my considerations almost as soon as I thought of them; however, my curiosity as to whether there exist men with almond-shaped testicles has lingered.

So my testicles, while not resembling closely any one species of nut, possessed enough similarities to nuts in general to make them more accurately called nuts than balls. Did being able to think about my body in this dissociated way, while clenched in agony at the base of Mrs. McCranie's pink azaleas, mean I was nuts? Though I considered it, I didn't think metaphor, elastic as it was, extended that far.

OR | Eric Ormsby

I don't have a single favorite word, but if I did, the supple conjunction *or* would figure high on my list. Of course, since it forms the first syllable of my surname, I could be accused of partiality. But in fact, I like and admire it for a score of reasons. It's not a showy word but a worker word, a syntactic functionary; and yet, for all its organizational aplomb, it secretly delights in nuance and ambiguity. *Or* stands like a squat bouncer at the revolving door of the disjunction. It bears the yoke of alternatives—"to be or not to be"—with all the robust orotundity of an ox. It summons its correlatives inescapably. Kierkegaard (the final syllable of whose name conceals a drawled Danish "or") orbits at the very edge of the horizon with his *Either/Or*. But *either* (whether you pronounce it as "eether" or "eyether") has the feathery feel of an insinuation while *nor*—that negative alternative in mufti—muffles the particle's bright opening vowel with the snidest of nasals.

Or is various in its intonations, especially when standing alone. Who can exhaust all the shades of defiant incredulity in an emphatic "Or?" Nietzsche resorted to this trick when he ended his early work *Morgenröte* (*Daybreak*) with the whimsical interrogative "Oder, meine Brüder? Oder?"—("Or, my brothers? Or?"). But the German *oder* (like the river which shares its name) carries a distinct whiff of the malodorous.

Or is splendidly homophonic. I always endeavor to load my rifts with *or*. And my writing hand, like Eliot's gaily responsive boat, ever strives to become "expert with sail and or." *Or* not only o'erflows the measure but is afterthought's most skeptical accomplice. (Or is it?)

The *Oxford English Dictionary*, which devotes several pages to this humble hinge of our tongue, tells us that it derives from "other." It notes that it has a temporal equivalent in *ere*. *Or* serves not only to balance alternatives on its sly pivot but to link words of identical meaning: Terre-neuve or Newfoundland. Even more, as the *OED* notes, it serves "the Boolean function of a variable," whatever that may mean. The dictionary doesn't tell us, though, how well *or* functions as the stuffing for grander words. An *orb* without its *or* is nothing but a sadly disemvowelled *b*. An *ordeal* dwindles sordidly to a deal. And what would *work* or *fork* or *rhetoric*—not to mention *word* itself—amount to but splinters of toppled consonants without that little hidden oriflamme?

It's pleasure to enunciate an *or*. The broad *o* demands a certain preparatory embouchure which alerts the lips and musters the mouth. It has, as I said before, a sturdy orotundity: it is *ore rotundo* (as Horace puts it), a syllable spoken "with round mouth." The vowel can expand; it muses, ponders, hovers before closing on the *r*, most diffident of American consonants. In a Mediterranean mouth, of course, that *r* positively clatters like an angry castanet when prolonged for dramatic effect: o-*r-r-r-r-r*! We refrain from such oratorical flourishes. Our *r* is the deference we pay to harsh choice; it bridles its brash *o* in exculpatory velvet.

The *OED* notes that *or* functions not only to demarcate alternatives but to make possible the "emphatic repetition of a rhetorical question." True to its monosyllabic modesty, this cunning particle plays the straight man to the jokester clauses it connects, but the core of the joke is in the *or*. Am I right or am I right?

This hard-working word has its share of false friends; sometimes, with the dimmest of echoes, it kibitzes on their glamour. In French, *or* means "gold." In Hebrew, it means "light."

PANTS | Nathaniel Taylor

Pants is a word that has always bugged me. I don't really have anything against pants themselves, although I try not to wear them when possible and they are also somewhat antithetical to *fuck*, my favorite word. My problems with the word *pants* are fairly simple. You can't pluralize it correctly, and I don't like the way it sounds.

Pants is defined most simply as a garment of clothing for the lower part of the body. It evolved from the older word *pantaloons*. *Pantaloons*, like *pants*, has the problem of being impossible to pluralize, but that's made up for by the fact that it is much more fun to say, and makes you think of old English peasants wearing loose-fitting pantaloons and perhaps doing a jig. According to some, the word was shortened to *pants* in the early to mid 1800s, creating, and I say this without hyperbole, the worst word in the history of language.

The plural form of *pants* is *pants*, and the singular form of *pants* is *pants*. If you take the *s* off the end, it becomes *pant*, which means something else entirely, to breathe in short quick breaths. The closest thing the word *pants* has to a proper singular form is the phrase "pair of pants," which bothers me because it sounds like you should be referring to a matching set of two pants, when you're actually referring to one single garment.

If you want to point out a specific pair to someone, you can't say, "Hey, check out that pants." You must say, "Hey, check out those pants." You don't do this with other words whose singular and plural forms are the same. You don't say, "Hey, check out those sheep," if you are only referring to one sheep.

Despite my hatred of the word *pants*, I am forced to use it, because *pantaloons* is simply too goofy for day-to-day conversation, and *trousers* is too serious and too British. It is this lack of alternative that maybe bothers me the most, although I think I just simply don't like words that think they're too good to follow the rules of the English language.

PERSONAL | Priscilla Becker

Recently I had occasion to revisit my skepticism about the word *personal.* I was up for a real teaching job, or so I thought, at an institution where I already teach as an adjunct. I didn't get the job, and my superior wrote me a consolation letter that included this sentence: "I know that doesn't mitigate the disappointment, but hopefully it will keep you from interpreting their decision as a reflection on their thinking of you personally or artistically."

The comment, though caring, is beside the point. When looking for a job, what one is really after is a job, not approval from peers. I won't go into the unintentional (I think) meaning that the selection committee failed to even think of me. But this is beside the point, too, because what I really want to figure out is why the word *personal* gets under my skin.

I'll start with my superior's comment: ". . . but hopefully it will keep you from interpreting their decision as a reflection on their thinking of you personally or artistically." Is there a way that thinking of me personally differs from just thinking of me? It sounds like it. I'd hate to think of certain hiring committee members thinking of me personally. The word *personal*, let's remember, is part of the phrase *personal hygiene*.

And I think it does have that cast—an intimate, sexual one; think of "the personals." I recently visited an online personals site (research!). The session started with a bunch of boxes of personal information to check off: *I am a (check) man seeking a (check) woman*—a status that could apply to roughly a quarter of the world. Checking off my statistics didn't seem very, well, *personal*. One of the meanings of *personal* is, after all, "bodily." Carrying something *on your person*. Now, that seems personal. But the virtual personals are the opposite of this—no body involved.

Many vacation spots are advertised as personal hideaways. The fact that they're being advertised seems to weaken the chances of their being either personal or hideaways. I'd be more interested in an *im*-personal vacation myself, one that didn't resemble my life at all. But maybe I am missing the point.

Personal differs from *private*, though these words are often used interchangeably, it seems. "That's personal" is a typical response to a question one would rather not answer. But I think "private" is closer, in this case, to what we mean; otherwise, there'd be a whole genre of writing called "the private essay"—full of personal details and anecdotes meant only for the writer, which, come to think of it, might not be a bad idea.

It seems the word *personal* modifies more nouns than it used to—personal trainer, personal checking, personal days, personal essay, personal knowledge, personal goals—and that not only the number of instances of the word *personal* has increased, but also its meanings. Many of these words at one time didn't need explication, such as *essay*. The term *personal essay* is a euphemism of sorts; it allows the writer to avoid the more explicit truth, "I write about myself." And perhaps this is a clue as to why the use of the word *personal* seems to have proliferated: because today, self-focus is hardly an exception. We accept, perhaps even demand, greater yield from this formerly limited word. *Personal*—pertaining to *me*—can modify just about anything.

There also seems to be something about the modifier *personal* that invites other modifiers, like *own*. "It is my own personal recipe" (indicating the inclusion of some secret ingredient no one but you could have imagined); "my own personal workout routine" (one designed exclusively for your, and only your, body); "We found our own personal getaway" (doubly tricky, it seems to me, as it indicates the getaway's perfection for the specific qualities of the particular couple, as well as a kind of sexual connotation—as though we're being teased to imagine the couple's own personal, intimate rituals). And look how the modifier *our* slipped in!

I suppose *personal* has evolved a meaninglessness, which is why it seems to invite other meaningless or redundant modifiers, like *own*. I mean, what does the word *own* do that *personal* does not, or *our*, for that matter? It intensifies, for one. Maybe if "our getaway" doesn't get your attention, "our own personal getaway" will. This wouldn't matter at all, of course, if we weren't prepared to look for services that fit our own personal needs. But we are, and so the conjuring of a private sphere is attractive.

Perhaps *personal* has been so stripped of meaning, of its personal nature, that it actually means just the opposite. I know it's bad practice to create an opposite by the negation of a word, but in the case of *personal*, I find there are two, slightly different opposites—one is *general*, the other im-*personal*. *General* is *personal*'s opposite when one wants to indicate something not specific, not of a particular body; whereas, *impersonal* is *personal*'s opposite when the idea is to convey coldness. Both opposites are alike in that they exclude the body. So the phrase *Don't take it personally* then means not to let it touch the body; or to keep it cold, outside. That's kind of lovely to think of. And if it weren't said so often, I could probably enjoy, at least intellectually, holding hurt at arm's length.

But when a day at the spa is billed as catering to your own personal needs, we're hovering on the brink of meaninglessness. I mean, how can your day at the spa be so different from mine? Mud packs, fluffy towels, exfoliants. But, again, perhaps this is the point—not to be an individual, but to be only as individual as the image of yourself.

For me, perhaps the most troubling usage of the word *personal* is the common phrase *Don't take it personally*, which always seems to remind me to take it personally. It's delivered on the heels of insult or bad news. To me, it seems part of a culture eager to dissuade you from your instincts, and hot to promote a pleasant distortion.

Recently a formerly private, and now that I have written this essay, merely personal use of a variant of the word *personal* came up in a conversation I had with my boyfriend. I was trying to explain how I felt about him. Eventually, after the usual inadequacies had been exhausted, and at a loss, I said, "I mean . . . you're my person." I was kind of surprised. I meant, of course, that he was my special person. But referring to him as my person has undeniably weird notes. That there could be a literal bodily confusion or a substitution in my mind of his physical body for mine seems very personal (perhaps unhealthy) indeed.

I think ahead to the day when I will be asked to dispose of my parents' personal effects, to sift through everything accumulated—meaningful, or not—over the course of their lives. I suppose the phrase *personal effects* makes me think of the word *effects* more than the word *personal*—the result, if you will, of their lives, the evidence of their time on this earth. I imagine I will have cause to consider a different kind of personal effect of my parents—everything they meant to me, and all the manifestations in my life of their presence.

But until then, I will go on with my skepticism—scoffing and clucking my tongue and getting offended at each misuse: I've brought it to a whole new personal level.

pREFER | Mark Noonan

Perhaps no word resonates more hauntingly across the hallowed halls of American literature than Bartleby's "prefer" in Herman Melville's story "Bartleby the Scrivener." *Prefer*: his implacable declaration of humanity in a society increasingly in contempt of individual choice and desire.

At first, all is well at Melville's No. __ Wall Street. Business is booming, and additional help is needed to copy in human hand the business and real estate contracts now flowing into the office. Enter Bartleby, "pallidly neat, pitiably respectable, incurably forlorn." For two days, this new lawyer's employee gorges on documents, "copying by sun-light and by candle-light." His lawyer employer is delighted—or should be, were it not for the sullen temperament of Bartleby. There is reason for this. After all, the lot of a human photocopy machine is a "very dull, wearisome, and lethargic affair," admits the narrating lawyer in the story.

The lawyer's other hired scriveners also display the disastrous effects of working at an occupation that alienates rather than rejuvenates. Turkey, in his sixties, can only function effectively up until noon. After that time, his face takes on a "florid hue" and his copying becomes blotched and unintelligible owing to "a strange, inflamed, flurried, flighty recklessness" that overtakes him. Nippers, a young man of twenty-five, is also stunted by this dead-end job. Once aspiring to learn the legal trade, he is beset now with dire credit and health problems that induce a "nervous testiness" and cause his teeth "to audibly grind together over mistakes committed in copying." In this Wall Street office, the effects of industrialization and capitalism at the expense of humanity are in full witness.

On just the third day of his employment, Bartleby has had enough. When called on to assist in clarifying a legal document, his "singularly mild, firm voice replied, 'I would prefer not to.'" Bartleby's reply offers a verb phrase dependent for its meaning on an absent yet understood active verb (*to copy*). This decided—yet decidedly open—response is our first hint that Bartleby's agenda is much broader than his boss could ever imagine. In these five short words, he intends to put a stop to the machine completely.

We hear the same siren call of resistance when Thoreau refuses to pay his poll tax in "Civil Disobedience." In Bartleby's defense of humanity there also echo the demands of Elizabeth Cady Stanton and Lucretia Mott's "Declaration of Sentiments" at the Seneca Falls Convention for Women's Rights. We hear the same in Huckleberry Finn's decision to break the law and "go to hell" in his bid to bring Jim into freedom, and in the decision of Ralph Ellison's Invisible Man to stay underground, and when Allen Ginsberg courageously puts his "queer shoulder" to the wheel of injustice in his poem "America." We may also remember William Lloyd Garrison's stirring words in protest of slavery in *The Liberator*: "I do not wish to think, or speak, or write, with moderation. . . . I am in earnest—I will not equivocate—I will not excuse—I will not retreat a single inch— AND I WILL BE HEARD."

America was founded upon natural law in opposition to authoritarianism. In "Bartleby the Scrivener" the figure of unjust authority is the nameless lawyer who narrates the tale. Recalling Jefferson's Declaration of Independence, which argues for consent of the governed, Bartleby ever so politely insists on his own sovereignty. And so, literature's most revolutionary war begins—a battle of words and will pitched in the claustrophobic, "walled-in" confines of a Wall Street office. Winners there are none. Bartleby's preference "not to" is, after all, a self-destructive suicide bomb, the shards of which remain embedded in us all.

QUIPU | Arthur Sze

Quipu means "knot" in Quechua and is "a device made of a main cord with smaller varicolored cords attached and knotted and used by the ancient Peruvians (as for calculating)." I became interested in quipus many years ago when I heard they might encode language. I discovered that numerical quipus followed a base ten system: the position of a particular knot might indicate 1s, 10s, 100s, 1000s. Different kinds of knots indicated the numbers one through nine, so a numerical quipu might serve as a valuable recording device: if it encoded potatoes in storage, it would contain vital information during a famine. Potatoes could be moved out of mountainside storage and used to feed people: a quipu knot could be untied and retied to keep the information current. A non-numerical quipu, however, might contain narrative information. A historical account describes how an Inca runner came to a village, and when he held up the quipu, the indigenous people joined a revolt in a nearby village against the Spanish.

I became more interested in quipus when I discovered ancient Chinese ones existed as well. In 2003, I hosted Dr. Tientai Wu, Director of the Institute of Ethnic Relations and Culture at National Dong Hwa University in Hualien, Taiwan, in Santa Fe at the Institute of American Indian Arts. Over lunch, I described how I was interested in Peruvian quipus, and, to my surprise, she told me how ancient Chinese quipus predated writing, and she wrote out four Chinese characters: *chieh sheng chi shih.* The four characters can be translated as "the record, or memorandum, of knotted cords." Although there is no book with this title, Dr. Wu told me the phrase refers to how the Chinese language existed before writing. Because the first two characters contain the silk radical, I surmised that ancient Chinese quipus were composed of spun, dyed, and knotted silk. Because these fibers are fragile, I also assumed that none of these quipus have survived. I began to research Chinese literature for references to quipus and discovered, with help from David Hinton, that in chapter eighty of *Tao Te Ching*, it says, "Let the people revert to communication through the knotted cords" (John Wu translation). And in Tu Fu's poem "Thoughts," he writes, "Someone started knotting ropes, and now we're mired in the glue and varnish of government" (David Hinton translation).

I pursued this interest and began to envision the process of creating a quipu. One begins with carding fibers (alpaca, cotton, or silk); they are spun clockwise or counterclockwise (in weaving, this is called a z-spin or s-spin); one creates a one-ply yarn; however, one could spin another one-ply yarn with a similar or opposite spin and yet spin the two together to create a two-ply yarn; furthermore, one could dye each ply the same or different colors. One could knot and employ different knots along the length of each cord that dropped from a main, primary cord. Suddenly the system became remarkably complex, sophisticated, and the possibilities were endless. Lightweight and portable, a quipu could be bundled up, carried in a pocket, and then pulled out and read.

I began to envision a book-length sequence of poems where the language was like spun, dyed strings and the repeated knotting included varying meanings of the same word. I looked up all of the dictionary definitions of the word *as* and, over time, incorporated most of them into a sequence. I liked the idea of elegant variation: repetition, but with shifts in meanings that would resonate and accrue over time. As this polysemous form of knotting evolved, I began to experiment with turning nouns into verbs, with syntactical knotting within a single sentence, and with anaphoric and epiphoric repetition. All of these elements were incorporated into my book *Quipu*.

RIFF | Ted Anton

A warm-up riff played by alto saxophonist Paul Desmond became "Take Five," one of the biggest jazz hits ever. A warm-up riff played by the trumpet section in the Tommy Dorsey orchestra became "In the Mood," a huge dance hit. When I played saxophone, my best work was in warm-ups, playing exactly what I meant to play, not trying to follow a tune.

When you mix thoughts at random—when you riff— you open yourself to a truth you would never have arrived at through logic. The elements bang up together by chance in a rush of ideas, and the chance juxtapositions take on a meaning of their own. The meaning is you.

Chance is God riffing.

Riff has been defined as "a short rhythmic jazz figure without melodic development," possibly derived from *refrain*, from the Middle French, meaning "to break back, or break again," as in a phrase or a verse recurring at regular intervals (*Webster's Third New International Dictionary*).

But I prefer to think of it as descending from *riffraff*, from the Old French *rif et raf*, and ultimately from *rifler* (to strip) and *raffler* (to snatch away), thus to *plunder* the dead after a battle.

A night dream is a riff.

Hip-hop sampling, when a pop phrase or a politician's quote is repeated randomly, is a form of riffing. In radio, when the producer rushes fast bits of quotes over and over for comic effect, it's called *shotgun*.

Riffing in basketball: desperately, in the game's final seconds, you throw away the plan, run every move you can, throw whatever it takes to make it to the hoop.

A shaman, says anthropologist Claude Lévi-Strauss, takes pieces of the natural world, eye of newt or paw of mouse, and mixes them together to create a broth or talisman of power, transforming the elements into a spell that may transform the world. Or is it only riffing?

Rif et raf, stripping "one and all" of the dead after battle, moved into English as "riff and raff," which meant to plunder "every scrap." This phrase appeared in Robert Mannyng's *Chronicle of England* (ca. 1338) and then in William Gregory's *Chronicle of London,* published in 1470. *Raffish,* signifying something lower-class and unconventional, was first used in English by Jane Austen in a letter to her sister Cassandra in 1801. Austen's letters were riffs on balls, clothing, people, etc.

Gene sequencing, analyzing millions of bits and pieces of DNA through an automated high-speed computer, deciphers a body's constituent chemical parts in a ten-thousand-line riff. The sequence of those elements accounts for everything in life, from my size to the color of my eyes to my propensity both to organize and to meander.

DNA, it could be said, riffs.

SIX-PACK | Thylias Moss

fork
flux
limited
mezzy
scale
simultaneity

FORK

To begin with what happens when saying *fork* in English, when a native speaker, to *limit*[1]

1. To be dealt with more fully later although *fullness* and *limit* may seem opposed unless contemplating a situation, such as existence, that is full of *limits*, which perhaps would be a waste of an opportunity to be full; an existence full of *limits* just outright seems incapable of exploiting *fullness*, well, fully. Of late, *limit* has taken on a link (difficult to *limit* or prevent associations when information is electrically imprinted in a neural network), the apparently *simultaneous* deployment of soft anchors to multiple neural information hubs, attaching another facet to each info group (*soft* because of their plasticity, their ability to be reworked, to bend, to expand). More research is needed here, more experimentation which certain funding sources would want to *limit* to non-human subjects, fearing monsters before the trials conclude

170

with, ideally, near-perfect methods and interventions that control how information is processed in the brain, maybe even a junk section that the *limited* thinker could empty through a programmable sequence of blinks and grunts. It would be great to see something emptying from the brain's disposal portal, to see a stream of junk info flowing out of a head into a sewer (the electrical discharge associated with emptying the junk bin perhaps could be amplified with some small —I'm thinking nano—device implanted somewhere in the nervous system, allowing the discharge to be simulated visually and/or sonically— maybe technology developed from the work that has resulted in the *vOIce* project *Seeing with Sound* in which the totally blind can see: http://www.seeingwithsound.com/).

this beginning further, speaks *fork,*[2] the upper central incisor teeth almost bite the *f* of the word into the lower lip, and air is forced through the opening.

> 2. **fork**: a language system that references multiple *simultaneous* operations; for instance: to think one way and behave in a different manner, to take a position inconsistent with established cues, clues, promises, trends, expectations; to deliberately establish cues, clues promises, trends so as to *fork* away from them; the love of deception; to stick that which is expecting something based on established cues with a *fork*; a pursuit-evading maneuver; to go one way then *fork* often abruptly in an unanticipated direction, foiling the pursuit; to be able to split, to be inhabited by *forking* personalities, each one of them capable of speaking *fork*.

As for *native speaker* —some clarification is needed here too, I suppose, for those of us (I mean me and others) with a sensitivity to the use of *native*:[3]

> 3. The *local*, not outside of the environment of this defining location; not an immigrant; undisputed, undisputable member of this, entitled by birthright, belongs in this incredibly *limited*[1] *forker girl's*[4]

>> 4. female practitioner of [11] *limited fork poetics*: the study of interacting language systems: any/all visual, sonic, olfactory, tactile systems/subsystems on any/all scales

clarifying reference tool kit[5]

> 5. that is: what these terms also look like in a mirror, specifically: gravitational mirroring,[6]

>> 6. subjected to an intensity such that there is displacement; the reflection as visual echo, reverberations of the deflecting encounter, a repositioning relocating the mirage, the dictionary and the anti-dictionary[7]

>>> 7. As on an episode of *Columbo*, his hair as black as deep space gravity can look, the black of gravity's effect in and near a black hole also a mirror; the episode in which a genius club member murders a rival genius by dictionary with the help of an umbrella and Tchaikovsky's overture to *Romeo and Juliet*.

> the mirage and its double, the meanings and the other meanings; the deviation that opens something, a little split so that meanings can be biopsied to determine what else, what they really contain

a term which isn't exactly double-edged, as *native*[3] has more than two edges, so is crystalline in structure, each edge further edged as magnification, beyond this text focus, can reveal; but I do mean specifically two edges, and the doubling of edge-intensity, so sharper effects[17] are achieved—even though positioning *on the edge* might be problematic, the apparently increased opportunity to fall off that edge, even if *edge* is a nod to the progressive—and such a fall is particularly problematic since no *drop-off range* has been indicated, so it would be a fall off the edge into nothing, and this is not the place, no matter how intense—or edged—the interest becomes to fall into a discussion of the physics and philosophical implications of a fall into *something* defined as *nothing*, *nothing* indicating some form of *negative space* even though landing in negative space is exactly where the use of *native* also arrives, *negative* as in *derogatory*, *negative* as in less than zero, outside of the range of what can be detected by the unassisted senses (including assistance with antidiscrimination legislation).[8]

8. consider the less-than-zero position in society of Ralph Ellison's Invisible Man, who says in the prologue:

> *I am invisible, understand, simply because people refuse to see me. . . . That invisibility to which I refer occurs because of a peculiar disposition of the eyes of those with whom I come into contact. A matter of construction of their inner eyes, those eyes with which they look through their physical eyes upon reality.*

Those sensitive (I mean me and others) might perceive (the perception encasing what is perceived in a reality, perception treating the object of perception as fact in the manner of its actual [in the *fact* of the manner of its] imprinting into neural networks where imprint sorting along a reality gradient does not occur) misuse in the usage being risked here;

a *native* speaker then, someone speaking a language as a first language of that speaker in a location where that language is commonly spoken, the language of the country of the person's birth, even if the language of this country is not the *native* language of that country, meaning not the first or original language of that country, but an imported language, as in a nonindigenous species that thrives (possibly via chokehold) in new surroundings whose threats successful against other species, perhaps other *native* species, are no threats to the transplant, so to speak English in North America is not to speak the language *native* to North America. The *native* languages, to use another out-of-fashion, out-of-taste, pretty much out-of-any-redeeming-value *value* of *native*, not even a redeeming mirage; the *native* languages of North America would be the languages of the *native* populations or *savages*, the uncivilized, designations easier to make if the tongue is *forked*, split,[9] able to speak from both sides of the mouth *simultaneously*,

9. the *forked* or *split* tongue suggests the possibility of torture technique to carry out the splitting, the work of single- or double-

edged splitters, such as the magic used to split Anderson's Little Mermaid's fish tail, reverberations and echoes of the split experienced each time she walks, splitting again the consequences of her decision into knives and *forks*, *utensils* that are *means* to access something, their purpose being to assist with access, as in extending access to higher social classes through use of the right *fork* with each course of the meal.

to state and contradict *simultaneously,* to juxtapose, to increase the likelihood of consistent indication of the presence of alternative, to more authentically represent the existence of multiplicity of meaning, to simulate justice through pointing to more than one way, to be pro-choice of expression, to be indecisive, unable or unwilling to commit to a single path, to extend the tongue's pickup ability through adding functionality similar to chopsticks, the *forked* tongue is also able to wrap its two serpent-prongs or tines around a single chopstick or similar stem so as to form a mouth-borne caduceus, a figure associated with healing; a *forked* tongue may also become a plaited tongue, a fashion statement in word and appearance.

To fork is to have more than one way to go, to split, to increase options, each one of which may be referred to as a *prong* or *tine*. *To fork* is to use a *fork*, possibly to create a system of bifurcations, possibly to choose a particular avenue of tine for some period of time. *To fork* is to use a *fork*, possibly to access something and make what is accessed usable by decreasing distance from what is accessed and the user of the *fork*. *To fork* is to lift. *To fork* is to dig into and possibly separate or filter with the branches or prongs. There is definitely the likelihood of loss, through the branches or prongs, of some portion of what is being accessed, what is being *forked up*. *To fork* is to support *with the fork*. *To fork* is to be at the location or to the location where something splits into more parts. *To split* is to divide into more parts; the earthquake *forks* the house, the bridge, the road. The coroner *forks* the cadaver in an autopsy. The broken bone is a *forked* bone. A yodel is a *forking* note. A tree is a bifurcating system of branches. A root system is a bifurcating system of branches. The bifurcated mandrake. A bifurcating system is a *forking* system. Each evolutionary branch and subbranch is an evolutionary *fork* or sub-*fork*. What a *fork* manages to lift is a *forkful* even if the *fork* is not at maximum lift capacity. The arm and hand system is a *forking* system. The digits or fingers of the hand are bifurcations or tines, usually articulated tines; a bird's foot, the articulated robotic hand of *The Terminator*;[10] the articulated robotic claw in those grab-a-toy mechanical gyp-boxes such as was in the lobby of my local Chi-chi's before closure and is still in the lobby of my local branch (*fork*) of the Quality 16 cinema chain (*forked* system) where *Limited Fork Poetics*[11] was born. *Tyne*[12] *Daly* is being inducted right now into a branch of the *fork* hall of fame. The twin (or two-pronged) towers of the World Trade Center system had a system of exterior *forks* as part of the structural and aesthetic integrity of the WTC.[13]

10. A film in three, to date, parts or tines (*forks*) featuring Arnold Schwarzenegger in a branch (or *fork*) of his career as the title character, from a *fork* of future that is also a *fork* of past, who attempts to create an alternative tine of future by using a present moment (the *now* in which the movie takes place) as a bifurcation point

12. *Tyne Daly* played Mary Beth Lacey, a detective on the television crime drama *Cagney & Lacey*; her star on the Hollywood Walk of Fame is marked by five bifurcation points (locations to which *forking* has arrived and/or locations from which *forking* can proceed). *Tyne* is the name of a river system in England. A *tributary* or *branch* of a river may be considered a *tine* of the river; such a river is *forked*. A *fork* in a road is a *bifurcation point*, a location where a road or segment of a road splits into at least one additional segment. *Tyne* is considered a variation, or branch, of *Tine* which is considered a branch or bifurcation of *Martina* and *Tina*. *Tine* is the name of a

Norwegian dairy producer, also Norway's biggest food company (at the time of this writing), a name that resonates (a bifurcating gesture or movement; the rippling water *forks*; branches of a *forking* system need not be straight and need not remain straight if they are or become straight for some length of time) in Norway as reference to *a bentwood box used in the seventeenth century and later for carrying and storing food, primarily butter and cheese.*[14, 15]

13. from http://911research.wtc7.net/mirrors/guardian/WTC/fig-2-4.jpg

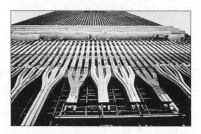

14. http://www.dmi.org/dmi/html/publications/news/ebulletin/ebvmarjg.htm

15. development of *Tine* logo; 3 bifurcations, next to *Tine Lady*, the face of Tine; both images *forked* (lifted, accessed) from: http://www.dmi.org/dmi/html/publications/news/ebulletin/ebvmarjg.htm

16. An image of a *fork* and spoon as seen at *tributenyc.org* (http://www.tributenyc.org/images/spoon-fork.jpg) recovered from the wreckage, probably from Windows on the World restaurant.

The eating utensil *fork* can be unforgiving, can bully the steak, the chicken, the prime rib; the eating utensil *fork* can hold the meat in place, prevent it from sliding on the smooth surface of a plate so that big meat can be cut down to pieces of a size easy to handle and swallow; the larger incarnation is a *carving fork* that holds in place bigger meat that will be cut, dissected into individual servings; *scissors*[17] are on an evolutionary branch of the *fork* family.

This consideration of *fork* has been *forking* in order to consider *fork*; this commentary has *forked* as literary device; when not a verb, when not involved in activity (see *flux*), when a noun, a *fork* is commonly a device or tool. The tines of a *fork* system need not be in direct contact with the handle or concept but can be; the branches of the *fork* may be linked to it remotely or through metaphor. There is no maximum number of tines that a *fork* may have. A *fork* may have both direct and indirect tines attached to it. Tines need not be linear. Each tine may support multiple bifurcation points. A maze or labyrinth is a *forking* system. The space between tines may be wide or narrow. Whether wide or narrow, the *fork* may lose something or some part of something to the spaces between. When the space between tines is sufficiently small, it may not be possible to perceive the presence of any space between the tines without the aid of instruments calibrated to measure on the scale of gap. When the space between tines is imperceptible on a scale of human aided or unaided perception, the *fork* may be considered as and may function practically as a shovel. A shovel plays less a role in *flux* than does *fork*. A *snow shovel* is usually a device to lift snow. A *snow fork* is a device or instrument that measures properties of snow.[18] A *snow fork* could also be a *fork* made of snow or a *fork* in which some of the tines are snow-covered for some period of time.

18. See a *snow fork* here: http://personal.inet.fi/business/ toikka/ToikkaOy/snowfork.pdf and read about how the *snow fork* functions.[19]

19. Footnotes are tines and subtines.

Many deadends are also tines.

A conjoined twin is a *forked* twin.

HD DVDs and Blu-ray discs are tines, one of which may remain open and likely to produce more tines, one of which may become a dead end.

A circular closed tine may also be hoop, ring, loop, feedback loop; a system of at least two closed tine loops can also be used to indicate infinity or the bones of a bow tie. Apple Computer's address, One Infinite Loop, is a *fork* of grab, the tines so close together they seem one, a fist, a *forkful* that is a handful, a hand closed around what a *fork* has grasped and not letting go; a palm reader reads *forks*, a palm reader navigates *forks*, a palm tree is a *binary fork system*, as are most trees: bifurcating roots[20] and bifurcating branches,[21] the apple, fig, coconut; fruit as bulbous tines, grapes as bulbous tines in clusters, wine as bulbous tines liquefied; the nervous system is a *forking* system as is *My Galactic Octopus*,[22] as is the nervous system of an octopus, as is an octopus.

20. A sewer system *forks*.
21. A ventilation system *forks*.
22. *My Galactic Octopus* was a selection in the 2007 Venturous Vanguard Film Festival and may be watched now on the *forkergirl channel* (http://www.youtube.com/forkergirl): http://www.youtube.com/ watch?v=V1Zu3v9zp_0.

FLUX

Sounds like the material itself, the word for the substance that is *flux*, a noun, an object whose shape is not nearly as defined as the word, the fluidity of the nature of *flux*, the elasticity of *flux*, the plasticity, the looseness, the space between the components of *flux*, the shape of generality, at the very least an advanced form of *flax*, an easily accomplished mutation, shape-shifting root of shape-shifting, and how lucky that this turn at this bifurcation point or *fork* is a turn toward an enabler of mutation, the constant state of *flux* or activity; the motion that so far the universe seems to be riding, shockwaves *forking* out in every direction noting the centerlessness of *flux*, reverberations of the big bang or of whatever the event was that got things moving, movement that has not ceased, an overriding shimmy, the collective aggregated wobble-states, not inertia, the band *Newton Flux*, the establishment of cycles, the sense of travel, intrinsic wanderlust, have existence: will travel, will move; glow and luminosity as movement, the *speed* of light, time, chaos theory, vibration, strings, sound, *flux* sounds like an energy drink, the energy, stamina to keep up, keep moving, how dynamic existence is, tireless, barhopping, name of a nightclub, name of a computer program, of the language to make the program do something, a *flux* of cards indicates a player adept in bluffing, a name of a placebo, a synonym for *synthesis*, brand name for the latest fake fat, a transit system: we are in *flux*, the transitions, the transitory stations in the movement arcs revealed when an action is revealed in slow motion; the transitions, the transitory movement revealed when inaction is revealed speeded up; *flux*, a time-lapse system that moves mountains, the shape of the universe, in *flux*: cyclic, a periodic bit of *flux* moving in the substance; *flux* is a comet, name of a future system of space travel, of the vehicle that travels deep space, another name for dark matter, to be in transition, the name for transitory existence, the breakdown of radioactive elements, where one is and remains while advancing by halves in Zeno's paradox, free-formed and reforming place, continuous change, the body is in *flux*, the economy is in *flux*, gas prices are in *flux*, political climates are in *flux*, the global climate is in *flux*, the rain forest is in *flux*, national boundaries are in *flux*, Palestine is in *flux*, Israel is in *flux*, morals are in *flux*, test scores are in *flux*, technology is in *flux*, *flux* is in *flux*, a physiological flowing as in diarrhea, as in dysentery, as in the bursting of the dot-com bubble (as if a **fork** had been stuck in it), the tumbling as in a clothes dryer: the clothes tumble in *flux*, the pattern of movement of debris in a vortex, the organized bait ball of a *flux* of sardines, the total electric or magnetic field passing through a surface, the *flux* mixed with a substance to lower its melting point, to melt: to go to *flux*, a *flux* of snowmen in the January thaw, a sad *flux* of Arctic and Antarctic ice, glacial *flux*, the process by which an event occurs, polite reference to promiscuity, some *flux* is also agitation, to be unable to rest, to stop, to cease to exist altogether; in *flux*, unable to get out of *flux* to be nothing, to not change form, to not decompose, to not aggregate, to not clump (the curdling of the universe into clusters and clumps of stars, star systems), to not smear, to do and be nothing, denial of an ending, grand procrastination, *flux*-tamer: a girdle, a shaper that forces a limit on midriff and abdominal bulge, brassiere, skin that changes shape as you do, the means through which that which is without intrinsic motion moves, what is in or on the car, in or on the earth, in or on the galaxy, in or on the universe, to stand still and move through time, the *flux* paradox: to move and go nowhere, synonym for the popping of static, for particle acceleration, swarm, dance: involuntary and voluntary forms, jitterbug, jittery bugs, pulses, moving from one to another, partnerships, relationships, ins and outs, pollination, propagation, a propulsion system, Æon

Flux (2005, film, moving picture): *Æon Flux* is the assassin that has been assigned by the underground rebels to change the course of mankind, forever. This is the story of her fight for justice, freedom, and revenge. Written by Cinema Fan (who writes plot summaries for films at the Internet Movie Database, a website in *flux*, wiki-content, *FLUX*: the Florida Linux User Xchange, *Flux*Europa: dark music and more, the news is in *flux*, tenure is meant to be anti-*flux*, heat transfer, matter transfer: *flux* as in transport phenomena, *flux capacitor*: the device in *Back to the Future* that enabled time travel, DeLorean upgrade, *Fluxus*: an intermedia movement whose making and thinking can have profound aesthetic impact; an artistic transport system, an antidote to aesthetic inertia in whatever gets made, to go with the flow, to collaborate with movement, the *flux* position of the Andy Goldsworthy's nature collaborations, sustained *flux*, though not constant for all that is *flux* apparently **simultaneously**, relative movement as various rates of movement, the sustained tendency for movement to occur on some **scale**, *flux*: a state of being in progress, humanity in *flux*, *flux* may flex, may be able to bend, warp, return to prior shape that is not identical for the return occurring at a different time, for a difference in energy output, acquisition, the big bang was also a big push, *f-lux*, function: luminosity, human luminosity perception, luminosity factor, *flux* as a vibrating (system of) tethers (dynamic **forks**, tines) that link constituents of the universe to each other, forming through the links a composite structure called *universe*, a wiki-universe, variation of *flocks*: groups/subgroups who believe that the sum of *flux* is the whole shebang.

LIMITED

. . . for it is known that there are boundaries whether or not the exact nature of a boundary is known at any given moment or can be known at some specified moment; indeed, the ability to specify a moment demonstrates a means of isolating a moment, of focusing on a moment, to discard what is not part of a specified moment, to exclude that which is not part of the moment being considered, to be able to exert parameters of confinement, to filter, to distill, to deal with specified parts, to develop and apply rules of focus, rules of concentration, parameters of inclusion, to be unable to exceed something, to be at capacity, not possible to go further, the inadequacy of knowledge, just short of cure, finite cap to any number of infinities within the borders, the point beyond which there is nothing, the privilege of being on the other side of nothing, exclusive, only for those with certain specifications, qualifications, restricted, location of power, wealth, pulls out all the stops, makes few stops along the trip, the laws that limit, that curb power, owners of a company legally responsible for no more than the capital invested, cannot be exceeded, the pinnacle, the best, for once and for all, the best film (etc.) to remain the best each year until a new film stretches the limit, raises the bar, otherwise, Shakespeare wins Nobel Prize for literature year after year after year, the line between possible and impossible, permissible and prohibited, a *limit* can be in *flux*, new data can push, revise, reassign *limits*, the *limit* of one circumstance is not necessarily the *limit* of any other circumstance, a *limit* may be shared, may be disputed, a speed *limit* can be exceeded, often with consequences, to exceed the *limit* of the speed of light is to have to rethink ideas that have exceeded the appropriate *limits* or brakes easily placed on ideas, becoming fundamental concepts instead, the foundation of other truths of existence, to be *limited*: to be without much talent or promise, consigned to be pretty much the way it is now, in need of air, water, nutrients, *limited* to need something outside of self.

MEZZY

First off: variation of *mezze*: a Mediterranean appetizer because
there is always hunger, some of which is for the *mezzy* of
existence, for essence, for the exceeding of apparent **limits**,
for a way to stretch, for exquisite, for elegant, for any purpose,
the spiritual *mezzy*, the *mezzy* art as a means of elevation, the
physical *mezzy*, visible architecture, structures, houses of *mezzy*
evidence, a restaurant in Oakland, the *mezzy* of poetry: the endless
feast for the insatiable appetite for meaning, luminous resonance,
toward zenith, little bits of tasty treats to please the palate,
syllables, stanzas, the delight of poem, planned or impromptu,
get some *mezzy* here: http://www.youtube.com/watch?v=
xmRI9YTyjrc&feature=related (*The* Mezzy *Factor*), here: http://
www.youtube.com/watch?v=MWLEBcOAa64&feature=related
(*The* Mezzy *Factor continues*), and here: http://www.youtube.com/
watch?v=L8VHrssxmRs (*The Inevitable* Mezzy *of Poetry*); the
mezzy of ability to locate and taste the delicious, to have no
significant **limit** to how much *mezzy* can be tolerated, to feast
today, to feast now and be full, extended, ascending, zenith-
bound only to have the sun set, to experience digestion,
the extraction of nutrients, shrinkage of the consumed,
the bounded, the **limited** via consumption of *mezzy*, to have
room for more *mezzy*, to make room for more *mezzy*, to need
to consume more, to be unable to exhaust the *mezzy* supply,
to be **limited** to seeking, desiring *mezzy*, popular *mezze* dishes
include: *babaghanoush, tabbouleh, rocket salad* (salatat jarjir),
kibbeh, shanklish, sausages that are treasure chests opened with
bites, *mezzy* menus that are on tables of content, search results
such as the menu of *mezzy* results when *Tokyo Butter* opens, the
Song there, the *mezzy* that sings, *Mr. Wilson's Cabinet of Wonders,*
Everything That Rises, Andrew Zimmern's bizarre foods, the
taste of everything, when *mezzy* morsels rot, when *mezzy* morsels
decompose, the result is more *mezzy*, maggot pilgrims come

to *mezzy* the *mezzy*, it cannot get putrid enough to completely wreck the *mezzy*, oh instead it can putridly enhance, there is the *mezzy* of putrefaction, the toxic is an edible idea, the *mezzy* of idea, taste of whole Google Earth, whole shebang food, what is possible to be ***forked***, a *mezzy* is a ***forkful***, the engine, the power of the universe, the fuel and the fuel burner is a *mezzy cooker*, whatever exists is a *mezzy cook*, to catch snowflakes on the tongue, to run through hordes of fireflies and locusts with the mouth open is to be *mezzy ready, mezzy receptive*, and a little bit of a beautiful fool.

SCALE

It's about time to *fork* this into perspectives, about time to
weigh and determine what's present, what's active according
to perspectives accessible without devices and with devices
designed to extend (within the *limits* of their making) what
the senses can access, it's time to *scale* this, remove those lime
deposits, the tartar on teeth, the tiles on butterflies, moths,
fish, preparing them for something else, to be of more use on
a human, a specific cultural perspective, let's supply context,
a way to order, a musical sequence, order of magnitude,
duration, to interpret, a way to check the reasonableness,
a table of feasibility, the various tracts and tracks of time,
relativity of perspective, dry skin, a basic feather, to *scale*: to
remove *scales*, to cross *scale* quickly, to move by *powers of ten,*
to use metaphor as a tool to cross *scale*, seeking symmetry,
seeking archetypal patterns on multiple *scales*, the repetition
of form in the universe, the redundancy of basic forms with
which to build endless variety, distribution, graphs, maps,
diagrams, the Mandelbrot set, *scale* models, in proportion,
chains, justice, measure, relative size, enlarge, shrink,
fractals, the repetition of propagation, *scale*, rate of change,
saturation, the temperature *scale*, increments of measure,
processing units, local events on a local *scale*, magnification
reveals *scale* toward the smaller, toward the larger, telescope,
microscope, tele-*scale*, micro-*scale*, impact, determination of
significance, insignificance and the relative meaning, impact
of these determinations on various and across *scales*, a tool
for setting balance, tone, *scale* factor for the expansion of
the universe, for the collapse, dimensions, the boundaries of
accountability, obesity monitor, a *scale* factor multiplies, the
perception of *wow* intensified, multiplied as Grant Williams as
The Incredible Shrinking Man shrank away, dissipated, the rate:
scale of his dissipation correlated to the rate: *scale* of expansion

of his awareness of the *scale* of this, his place value, the scale
of placement of exponents, superscripts, approximations,
greater than, less than enclosures, how something is seen, how
something can be seen, alternative representation of the same,
of similar information, packaging, integrity manager, what is
being considered, what is available, *scale* of the undertaking,
of the menu, ratio, Fujita *scale* of tornadic activity, Beaufort
scale of wind activity (includes reference to horse heads which
scale for me a silhouette that embraces *fiddles*, and the related,
on that *scale*, treble clef of seahorse), the Saffir-Simpson scale
of hurricane intensity, to be *scaled*, to be evaluated, rated,
assigned a relative position, family of man (includes these
forks: women, children, ~97% of chimpanzee DNA).

SIMULTANEITY
Stop right here •
Simultaneity should not be last •
If *simultaneity* exists, it is not last •

So while a linear *scale* managed progress through the layout of these definitions, in truth, *fork, flux, limited, mezzy, scale, simultaneity* existed concurrently on different scales, at different rates of changes, different levels of perceptibility, different and multiple locations; all have been present in some form(s) in some location(s).

The pattern of distribution of these elements is not necessarily linear, but any *flux* portion *forked* for examination may be perceived or momentarily *limited* to parameters of investigation in which a linear assessment makes sense and on the *scale* of circumstances being considered, *linear* behavior manifests, holds true for calculations and observations while at the same time, in a larger consideration, on a different *scale,* assessments may need adjusting, for what works, what makes sense, what has truth and *mezzy* on a particular scale may fail, that failure offering a *mezzy* of failure, as *scale* shifts, what makes sense shifts, what has truth shifts, *mezzy* shifts; the *mezzy* constant is the existence of, the persistence of a form of *mezzy.*

Is it that the forms of what exists on each *scale* on which something exists are necessarily changing? No.

Just watching it can change its behavior.

It probably has behavior without being watched.

But one possibility of *simultaneity* is that of consensus, that of

188

conspiring to maintain the *simultaneous* existence itself; the collective exertion of belief in the shared existence projects that existence, that *limit* of what is; the *mezzy* of collaboration, for everything existing to manifest some element, some evidence (presently detectable by others or not, whose development of tools to detect presences is usually constrained by the ways in which those developers have been shaped by perceiving to seek [perceptible] evidence) of presence on some *scale* for some period of time, measured according to some perspective, on some *scale* so that there is no universal time for the *simultaneous* manifestation of presence.

Simultaneity then suggests occurrence during a shared unit of time, the length or duration, the experience of the shared unit differing according to the perspective of the constituents sharing the unit of time; it isn't even the same time on earth, separation of hours, of degree, *scale* of light, darkness; for some hours (relative to a computation of *hour* in this solar system on this planet) of a day (relative to a computation of *day* in this solar system on this planet in this galaxy in this universe) it isn't even the same day on earth, all inhabitants of earth do not use the same calendar; from each *scale*, from each perspective, there is a different implication of *simultaneity*.

I do like *the starburst model of simultaneous acceleration of the known universe, the universe in which there is some trusted evidence of occupancy, other universes, which may exist simultaneously, at this moment (scale of time) existing speculatively, existing in hopes, wishes, imagination so is real there, in the realm of* **limits** *of mind, existing if not exactly parallel, then with the external mostly-three-dimensional (it seems) universe; I do like the shape of that more-or-less uniform expansion, the idea of growth in all directions, with little detectable discrimination, as eager a move toward heavens as toward hells; I do like the*

189

*distribution of growth occurring as air imparts growth to a balloon, and while there may not be precisely equitable distribution of debris if and when the balloon bursts, if the balloon model of universe is accurate; while there may not be equitable distribution of debris if and when the balloon bursts, I envision a **mezzy** of curved, of eccentric **fork** tines; I envision a luminous chrysanthemum of petals and flowers extending in arcs and curves, bends, luminous warps and displacements, forever fading, forever fizzling, dropping seeds, manufacturing more cool, way cool universes, antiverses.*

SOLMIZATE | Cole Swensen

Solmizate: to sing any object into place. Most literally, it's singing by the syllables of the do-re-mi-fa-so-la-ti-do sequence. That's all it may be, literally, but I happened to get introduced to the word with a slight error in it—one of those errors that is, in fact, an errancy, a wandering off from the beaten path, and, as with the "knight-errant," the "word-errant" also has something inherently noble about it. It is off on a mission to create more meaning in the world. In the case of this errant word *solmizate*, I first heard it used to describe the process of singing the birds on a bank of telephone wires as if they were notes on a musical staff, an endless composition that keeps refining itself with the coming and going of the flock.

By extension, this image seemed to suggest that any object has an inherently musical relationship with those objects around it, and that any given scene, say, the one framed by a window, is its own orchestra, quartet, duo, depending on what's going on out there. Through solmization, all objects have a voice, which changes in relation to the others around it, some coming together in chords, others in discord.

Errancy operates yet another way in this situation and introduces another of my favorite words, *constellation*. If we look out the window and try to sing the birds on the telephone wires, we're effectively collapsing a three-dimensional space into a two-dimensional one. Yet if we don't, if we refuse that collapse, and instead accept depth as a new musical value in order to account not only for birds on wires farther away but also other things—a tree branch, a distant chimney, a passing airplane—that enter into the scene, we end up with a spherical music that creates new relationships in the way a constellation does, as it takes one star from Galaxy A, another from Galaxy C, and so on, and makes of them a new system while leaving them still functioning in their old ones.

In the long fight to dethrone linear thinking from its default position and come up with other ways of arranging the world, the constellation offers a nice alternative in its complete flexibility. The problem, one could say, is that the constellation principle offers too many possibilities—how do we decide which disparate elements to bring into new systems? Here, solmization offers a guiding principle. We choose those that make beautiful music.

STILL | Robert Mueller

The word *still*, so obvious a choice for all purposes, will always have appeal that the moment itself, as pause and as relief, just by its being, will have for the poor soul troubled and almost too weary of sensibilities. It is a word in English for all climates, crafted and quick and tampingly of Germanic-family base. Monosyllabic and sure and strong, though a helping word, it bears familiar two-pronged marks of breaching consonant-combo *st* and doubling, un-doubting, restful *ll*. *Still* means and realizes multiple aspects, the feeling of what is sifted and safe, what rilling and quiet and constant, what comes back again welcomingly, and what is sure-fire prescription and impression, playing all the quieting parts. It is adjective, adverb, verb, and as *stillness*, noun. It fills the line, also quietly, but can drop and end and rhyme the line in clarity and simple belief. Though obvious and for all purposes, not achieving, almost never reaching the highest merit, more blend than beacon, it nonetheless comes home. It tarries, it bends, it buds. *Still* steps in when the person may cherish, may side to it, when she may adopt, he touch, lightness and leaf.

With some words, to keep staying power, you stake your life on the image and matter, if only for a moment. Thus those who figure, those who dress it up, but who drift in tendency, may yet flourish, in brief, and may pluck and shim inside protected chase. They are at it still, the qualities remain there still, the unblocked harbor of what is left. The way is not always *ignis fatuus*; it may one day share place and level pleasure and approach, be where it leads in times expected or unexpected, in phases now ballooning, now steadying. So you feel its use, its pace. You know and live the passion calmed in the mere word's cusp. You tend to it in and through. But is the word perhaps also a too-frequent visitor? Can the altering play indifferent still? Oh yes, oh yes, the place obtains, there is this beaming confidence, and sometimes there is not one better. Sometimes the power to calm leaves well enough clear, sometimes alone and dear it traces uneventfully.

SUBITANE | John Taggart

Subitane, meaning "sudden": Latin-derived, somewhat exotic. First come upon in the thickets of etymology while working on a translation of Sappho's first fragment. The fragment is sometimes given the title "Hymn to Aphrodite." It is in any case an Aphrodite poem, a love goddess poem, and something of a prayer or a beseeching (by Sappho, by a mortal) to the goddess. It has been many times translated. In an effort to avoid repeating, merely altering previous translations, I sought out the roots of the Greek words. This was done primarily in Pierre Chantraine's magnificent *Dictionnaire étymologique de la langue grecque*. Chantraine is assiduous and suggestive. So one, pursuing Greek, is soon in a tangle of that language, French, Latin, and several others. Such research amounts to submarine work. Thinking of that and of how the goddess (her birth) has been portrayed, the word becomes linked with water, a feminine body in or emerging from water. She is not standing on a half-shell above water but in the water. She is a diver floating up from her dive, body arched, head held back and hair streaming out, just breaking the surface of white froth and bubbles. The water

195

beneath the surface is dark, black. The body is crisscrossed with lines and patterns of light. The skin of the body is finely pebbled from the water. The diver's emergence occurs suddenly. To use another word for the experience (the encounter) of the figure of this word: it's "sublime." It's sublime "in the old sense" (as Pound said). Both beautiful and terrifying, rather more than what could be expected, the unexpected bordering on the shocking. With Sappho and the goddess in mind, then, like love itself.

SW*EET* | April Bernard

Because of the long *e*, this is a word that forms the mouth into a smile—not a grimace, as *ea*, *ei*, and *ie* do—just a small expression of pleasure at the tasting of a drop of honey. The final *t* twits a chirp, a bird call.

My son, who is eleven, says "Suh-weet!" when he means all sorts of things, from "How nice," to "Got away with that one!" to "Unfuckingbelievable!" This is not remotely distressing to me, since I know the word will hold up through this generational mangling just fine. After all, *cool* still remains *cool* in all its central meanings, though it no longer means, I don't think, "I'm saying this word because I don't have anything else to say."

Sweet and *deep* and *green* are the three best words in English. They make a late-spring copse, a greensward sloping into a ha-ha, the smells of a hundred flowers, mimosa and gardenia and jasmine, tiny buds crumpled for the released sweet scents of lavender and honeysuckle and the resin of spruce onto your fingers.

As a genre, the pastoral is forever sweet, for although there is death in Arcadia, the blood of Adonis spills green and turns to blue anemones that always smell sweet with spring that does, reliably, return. Drink some mead from the carven cup, have another piece of cheese, and sing another song. Pan's pipes come from the sweet reeds he clutched when Syrinx escaped his grasp. He blows into that sweet girl now, all that lust made sweet by song. "Suh-weet, Suh-weet," sings the phoebe, the towhee, and the cardinal, according to the various bird books on my shelf. Like my son, the birds sing sweetly, and they sing sweet.

Sweet is a word beyond metaphor, the sweet thing itself.

SWEETIE | Lawrence Raab

My first idea was to choose a word that has led me—and might again lead me—to those unpredictable leaps of thought a poem generates when it begins to find its shape. *Wind*, perhaps, might take me there, or *dark*, or *alone*. Or something more abstract—*tenderness*, perhaps, or *nostalgia*. Or, as my wife usefully suggested, *perhaps*. But no, I wanted a word I could think about as *spoken*, intriguing because of the ways it could be said by one person to another. So I thought of *sweetie*.

It's hard to imagine *sweetie* not surrounded by quotation marks, as well as accompanied by other words that establish tone, and so reveal the emotional life of the moment. In the sentence, "My sweetie was dancing on the lawn," our attention is drawn to the way the speaker feels, an affection that more or less vanishes with "My girlfriend was dancing on the lawn." (Perhaps he's embarrassed now. It's late. She's drunk. Or she's both drunk and so beautiful that everyone left at the party desires her, and he knows it, and so does she. This is a story about jealousy. Or it could be.)

And if you were to read in another story, "His sweetie was dancing on the lawn," you'd wonder not so much about the "he" or the "she" but the narrator. What right does he have to use the word *sweetie,* unless, of course, he's no omniscient narrator at all, but a *someone* with a voice and an attitude? (Another tale of jealousy presents itself.) *Sweetie* always has an "I" behind it.

When I thought of the word, I thought of that sort of presence, and of tone—the way tone of voice embodies and conveys emotion. I thought of a certain kind of intimate affection—not the gusts of passion, but the ease of tenderness. I thought of how every day I use the word *sweetie* dozens of times— to my wife, Judy, to my daughter, Jenny, to my dog, Molly, who knows what I'm feeling only through the way I speak.

Of course *sweetie*—like *dear* or *darling* or *sweetheart* or for that matter most words—can be turned on its head, emptied of endearment to display something bitter. "We should have left the house an hour ago, *sweetie,*" suggests strain and impatience. *Sweetie* hangs uncomfortably at the end of that statement, perhaps in italics, to make the point that things are really not going at all as sweetly as they should. Move *sweetie* to an even more unnatural place in the sentence—after *house,* say—and the effect is intensified. Leave *sweetie* out of a sentence where it is used to having its snug and comfortable place, and that absence conveys worry, or disappointment, or anger. When "Good morning, sweetie," becomes merely "Good morning," it's not so good, which both of us know.

In its unironic mode, *sweetie* is *sweetheart* dressed casually. It's off-handed but earned, appropriately taken for granted, at least for the moment. The word sounds good, slipping into the sentence at the right moment. It's like a tasty, though not particularly exotic, piece of candy, which is what it originally meant—not a someone but a confection. The child was charmed by a sweetie before she became one. And a "sweetie wife," the *Oxford English Dictionary* notes, was not a particularly adorable companion but "an itinerant vendor of gingerbread."

Sweetie is also the name of at least one band, innumerable candy shops, an "array" (according to Google) of "cute and clear icons to use in your nifty web application," and the first movie by Jane Campion, which I've never seen. But I remember encountering the title and thinking: what a good title that is. Why? Because the word all by itself suggested the presence of point of view without revealing what it was. The ordinary became problematic, even a little mysterious, which is another word I was tempted by, though I'm always tempted by what's not known, not fully understood, by that moment when the familiar slides a little closer to the strange.

"Sweetie," I can hear him saying, "come back inside the house. It's late. Aren't you tired of dancing out there all alone on the dark lawn? Yes, perhaps I've missed the point again. You're trying to tell me something and I just don't know what it is. Sweetie, is that it? *Sweetie?*"

THERMOSTAT | Michael Martone

I touch it every day, a secular mezuzah at the threshold of climatic change. On the wall, at eye level, a floor above the furnace it regulates, it is connected and remote. A hemispheric sconce embossed with the proprietary brand on its clear bubble: HONEYWELL. With the tread of my fingertip, I nudge the clear cleats of the inner ring delicately, dialing a safe, toward the triggering calibration of the two fine red needles, one below indicating, its shadow falling upon the numbered scale, how it feels and the other, on top, quivering as it inches toward the desired state.

Henry Dreyfuss designed it, just another mechanical object in the stream of streamlining. Modern to imagine everything smoothed, rounded, shaped by a constant manipulation. The wearing away. Friction as artist. All this metal in our hands pliant, malleable, plastic even, warmed to the touch, to the point of melting, molded into these organic solids of French curves so that even the most inanimate of things looked (when not moving) to move. Everything designed for speed, molting molecule by molecule, thin peelings of skin, a response to the

202

constant abrasion of invisibly moving air. The rubbing away. The erasure to the point of sculpted, cupped parentheses. Perfectly still but still in motion.

Thermostat. Heat, of course, but in "stat" cleaves both the sense of immediate, the "stat" of televised code blues, and the "stat" of passive regulation. Stationary. Statistics. Standstill. The instrument for feedback. As is skin. A touch. A response to touch. The shiver. The twitch. The gooseflesh. The blush. Mine is anodized. Beneath the cowling, the mechanism of static. The watch spring and the bulb of quaking quicksilver that trembles on its mirrored surface, responding to the eddies of my breath and, when I stop breathing, to the reverb of my heart transmitted through the cold air.

I touch it, and touching it I ease the imagined temperature past the ambient one. At that moment, deep in the house, I feel sound like the distant launching of mortars, an inhalation of air as the oxygen in the room around me is drawn down the returns, the jets of blue flame igniting somewhere.

TOPSOIL | Mary Swander

I flip over the weed-slicing blade on my *gartenblechle*, or rotary cultivator, and sink the shoes down into the rich, black garden earth. My palms wrapped around the oak handle, I push the cultivator back and forth across my 20 x 30-foot plot, loosening and lifting the soil. Across the valley, my Amish neighbors, the Yoders, are out in their garden performing the same ritual. A mother and her two daughters work side by side—specks on the horizon. I squint into the distance, and the red kerchiefs tied around the daughters' hair are dots on a divided, two-toned canvas: the black ground curving to meet the enormous blue sky. The Yoders have taught me to use the *gartenblechle*, rather than a wasteful gas-powered tiller. They have taught me to come out here each spring, to reach down and pinch the garden soil, testing its moisture and readiness for the plow.

My garden plot sits prominently in the middle of my acre of land in the middle of the largest Amish settlement east of the Mississippi River. I live in an old Amish one-room school-house, the swing sets and ball diamond back-stop still standing watch over the slow roll of the buggies up the road in front of my door. My garden perches atop a gently rolling hill that looks down on a valley dotted with white farmhouses, red barns, and lush green fields worked with horses and 1940s vintage tireless tractors. The fields are planted in a rotation of crops: corn, beans, alfalfa, and oats. Up and down the road, the Amish and Mennonite women work their own gardens that are both practical and artistic. The clean, straight rows that feed families of ten are ringed with borders of bright red cannas, orange cosmos, and yellow marigolds. Pink roses climb trellises and white clematis winds up around the poles of the purple-martin houses.

Yet in the spring, this landscape is but a sketch. The garden vines teeming with blossoms and budding vegetables, the trellises burdened with brightly colored flowers, all need to be detailed with a finer brush. To complete the painting, the gardens and farms need to develop. To thrive, the crops need adequate rainfall, proper temperatures, proper care, and proper soil. Situated between two fertile riverbanks—the Mississippi on the east and the Missouri on the west—Iowa is home to some of the most fertile topsoil in the world. In the spring, a glance downward from an airplane reveals field upon unrolling field of exposed topsoil—dark, brown, and moist— ready and waiting for the plow.

❖

Soil is composed of mineral and organic matter, water, and air. The actions of wind, rain, ice, and sunlight break down rock into smaller particles ranging in size and texture from clay and silt to sand and gravel.

If I were able to sink my bulb planter all the way down through the many layers of soil in my garden, through layer upon layer of rock, I would hit Precambrian bedrock, one to two billion

205

years old. On top of the Precambrian rock, the successive layers of rock deposited at earlier times contain fossils that document a land that was periodically covered in shallow seas. Fossils in the Cambrian rocks, approximately 500 million years old, depict a life limited to primitive forms: trilobites, algae, and brachiopods. About 450 million years ago during the Ordovician period, a warm, shallow inland sea once again covered the area. Sea sediment formed a diversity of rock types and of life, including algae and major invertebrate groups: corals, mollusks, and echinoderms like the beautiful crinoids.

When the seas retreated, erosion most likely shaped the land, removing some rock and marine sediments. But by the Devonian period, 413 to 355 million years ago, once again limestone, dolomite, and other rock types formed from sediments of ancient seas. Vertebrate animals made their debut. Sharks and bony fish floated through the same waters with brachiopods and lower life-forms.

The Mississippian period, 310 to 355 million years ago, saw the last of the widespread ocean waters to wash across the interior of what is now the North American continent. The sediment rocks of this era, primarily limestone, contained rich quantities of fossils, particularly crinoids. The Mississippian seas finally receded and exposed a large, emergent land mass, once again open to weathering and erosion.

Huge coal swamps covered much of southern Iowa during the Pennsylvanian period, 310 to 265 million years ago. A tropical or subtropical climate gave rise to a different set of species: scale trees, club mosses, seed ferns, cockroaches, snakes, and large amphibians. A lack of tree rings in fossil remains suggests that the region enjoyed a perpetual summer of warm and moist days, absent of distinct, changing seasons.

From the Permian to the Cretaceous periods, 265 to 130 million years ago, the warm, moist climate turned drier. Iowa was most likely above sea level, and the region is thought to have been a low, arid or semi-arid plain. Again, shallow seas washed over the land, and deposits of shale, lignite, conglomerate, and limestone formed the Cretaceous bedrock. Primitive coal-swamp plants were replaced by the forerunners of familiar trees that dominate today—such as magnolia, poplar, sassafras, willow. Although their fossils have never been found in Iowa, this was the era of dinosaurs that took to the land, water, and air. Fossils of gigantic flesh-eating reptiles, and of giant turtles and crocodiles, have been found in the state and can be traced to this period.

The Tertiary period, 65 to 2.5 million years ago, ushered in a climate that is recognizable today. The North American land mass that had previously been located near the equator drifted slowly northward into its present-day location. The climate became cooler, drier, and less stable. Humid, subtropical flora gave way to savannas and savannalike parklands. Fossils of seeds and other plant materials stuck in the jaws of an ancient rhinoceros are the earliest predecessors of today's prairie grasses. Fossils of other large mammals—from the cat family, to horned ruminants, to camels—suggest the land was an open savanna similar to those found in Africa today.

Toward the end of the Tertiary period, a huge shift began. The mean temperature of the region dropped, and large masses of ice and snow moved southward from the North Pole, covering what are known today as the Midwest and the Great Plains. During the last Ice Age, beginning 2.5 million years ago, ending just 10,000 years ago, the temperatures warmed, then receded, the ice melting, then again moving southward over the land, over all the layers of bedrock that had been laid down since the Precambrian period. The glaciers deposited their till on top of the land, and these sediments—sand, clay, and pebbles—were left to weather and erode for tens of thousands of years. Undoubtedly, the till mixed with other wind-blown and water-borne particles to form what we recognize as soil today.

❖

Air and water fill the gaps between the larger particles. Plant roots bind particles together and raise minerals from deep in the ground. Plants and their remains form food for burrowing insects and earthworms.

My great-grandparents homesteaded in Iowa shortly after the Civil War. They had fled Ireland in the wake of the Famine and were searching for good soil. They set out with thousands of Irish, Germans, Scandinavians, Czechs, Welsh, Scots, French, Amish, and others to find a place where they could build a cabin, a barn, keep a few chickens, sow a field of wheat, and, yes, plant a few potatoes in a garden. They set off across the Mississippi River to find themselves in a sea of prairie flowers and grasses, vegetation with roots that sank deep into the ground.

Homesteading journals often record the astonishment of the pioneers when they encountered the tallgrass prairie. A horseback rider could be swallowed up by the grasses, the grasses that stretched from horizon to horizon, the grasses that to these Europeans looked like weeds, worthless in a flat landscape, beautiful with their varied textures and colors, but there to be cleared and plowed up to make way for farmland.

Big bluestem, Indian grass, and prairie cord grass. Little bluestem, prairie dropseed, porcupine grass, sideouts grama, and needlegrass. The grasses mixed with the prairie flowers to create a rich, dense cover of vegetation. Purple coneflowers, black-eyed Susans, smooth blue asters, partridge peas. The prairie grasses and flowers provided cover and food for hordes of insects, birds, and small rodents. In the more modern arid climate, the water-loving rhinos of ancient times gave way to buffalo, animals that grazed the grasslands and, in turn, provided food and shelter for the indigenous people.

Clumps of bird's-foot violets turned the hillsides blue as the sky. The rough-leafed green grasses soon gave way to the yellow puccoons, sweet williams, scarlet lilies, shooting stars, and later the yellow rosinweeds, Indian dye-flowers, and goldenrod. The skies were filled with birds, great eruptions of geese, ducks, herons, and cranes, their feathers shining in the sun, lighting down on the rivers, marshes, sloughs, bogs, and fens, the remnants of the shallow seas of the ancient past. Prairie dogs, wolves, bobcats, badgers, deer, foxes, coyotes, and ferrets lived in grasses and savannas with frogs, toads, snakes, and fish populating the waterways.

The rich black earth of the prairies was the product of the thick grasses and abundant animals that populated the region. Over a course of thousands of years, the prairie grasses and animals died and returned to the soil, enriching it, acting as a renewable compost, building the ground into ever more fertile land with each successive year. Pioneer farmers liked to boast that prairie soil was so rich that it could grease the axles of their wagons. They were stunned by the soil's fertility, but what they didn't always recognize was its long geological history—and its fragility.

❖

When bacteria and fungi decompose the dead plants, animal droppings, and dead animals, all convert into dark, fertile humus. The top layer of earth, dark and rich in organic matter, is called topsoil. It varies in depth from 8 to 45 cm and is tilled in the cultivation of gardens and farm fields.

Ironically, the fertile soil of the prairie was its undoing. In the words of Herbert Quick (1861–1925), son of pioneers,

"Breaking prairie was the most beautiful, the most epochal, and most hopeful, and as I look back at it, in one way the most pathetic thing man ever did, for in it, one of the loveliest things ever created began to come to its predestined end."

In a space of less than 100 years, Iowa became the most cultivated state in the Union. The native prairie grasses and flowers disappeared. Now less than 0.1 percent of Iowa native prairie remains. Scattered remnants can be found in the waves of corn and soybeans that have replaced the ancient seas of the past. Some roadside ditches, pioneer cemeteries, and railroad beds across the state still blossom forth in August with purple coneflowers and black-eyed Susans. These lone sentinels tell the story of an ancient geological process that has come to an abrupt stop.

Each time I lower the shoes of my *gartenblechle* into the garden ground, I am turning over topsoil—the top layer of dirt. The bottom layer is Precambrian bedrock. Topsoil is made up of minerals, organic matter, water, air, and living soil organisms. Topsoil is the root zone, the place where the plants absorb water and nutrients. Beneath topsoil lies the subsoil, full of nutrients and less rich in organic matter, but less penetrable to plant roots.

Not only has most of the prairie vanished, but most of the topsoil has been depleted from the Plains states. One hundred and fifty years ago, the topsoil in Iowa was twelve to sixteen inches deep. Now it is six to eight inches deep. Over the course of geological time, it takes 500 years to create one inch of topsoil. The current rate of loss is ten to fifteen tons per acre per year. Each time the soil is plowed and left bare and open to wind and rain, some of the topsoil erodes.

When I was a child, my grandmother drove me past the home place, the farm that she had eventually inherited from her homesteading parents. My grandmother told me how she had tried to address the problems of the past, how most farmers had planted monocrops—mostly corn—year after year, then, during the drought and heat of the Dust Bowl, had watched tons of their precious topsoil lift up into the air and blow away.

The crop rotation in which my grandmother and others engaged during the 1940s through the 1960s helped to replenish the soil. They followed the lead of the Amish and rotated one dissimilar crop after another in a field. The rotation helped to avoid the build-up of pathogens and pests that tend to proliferate when the same crop is planted repeatedly in the same field. Crop rotation also works to replenish the soil nutrients depleted after any harvest. But the industrial agricultural boom of the 1970s ushered in another era of monocropping, and put an end to most four-crop rotations and manure spreaders. Farms became larger and more mechanized, with most operations moving toward two crops only: corn and beans.

Today, most farming is achieved with heavy applications of chemical fertilizers, herbicides, and pesticides. The topsoil becomes depleted of earthworms and is less healthy. A depleted soil needs even more chemical fertilizer, and so the cycle repeats itself. With the recent surge in ethanol, farmers have begun to abandon even a two-crop rotation and have headed into planting "corn on corn." The Midwestern landscape is once again becoming vulnerable to the kind of erosion experienced during the Dust Bowl. Still, methods of sustainable agriculture are making progress, emphasizing the need to maintain the natural fertility of the topsoil through practices such as crop rotation and natural fertilizers.

❖

The root systems and organisms of Iowa's past vegetation—prairies, marshes, bogs, and fens—transformed the raw mineral deposits into an invaluable natural resource.

But why should we care? Once, during the farm crisis of the 1980s, I was interviewed by a reporter for ABC News. "Why should a viewer in New York City care about farms?" he asked. "Because New Yorkers eat," was my first response. There's an obvious practical connection between producers and consumers. "But why should anybody care?" the reporter kept asking.

Why should we care about farms? I thought. Why should we care about the people living on them, the people that the farms feed, the ecosystems that farms have destroyed? Why should we care about the rich soil that was formed through millions of years of change and wonder, the folding under of all the flora and fauna that had thrived on a continent that had drifted through space and time? Why should we care about those brachiopods, those flesh-eating reptiles, those coal swamps, those prairie flowers and grasses? Why should we care about bedrock, about subsoil, about chemicals and fertilizers, about the destruction of earthworms? About topsoil? Why should we care about dirt?

The Amish used to roll their dead up in sod and lower them into the ground for burial. For dust thou art and unto dust thou shalt return. "You can compost anything," my neighbors, the Yoders, often joke. We care about the soil because we eat, but we also care because we are part of a much larger process, one of being, of loss, of decomposition, of losing ourselves to become part of a bigger whole, a substance that will eventually bring renewal and life to others. Someday we too will be folded into the earth, we too will become part of the soil.

UMAMI | Yong-Woong Shin

In 1908, Kikunae Ikeda, a Japanese chemist, identified the fifth basic taste, "savory," and named it *umami*. He discovered its chemical basis, glutamate, which he isolated, patented, and had canned into Ajinomoto, "essence of taste," flavor enhancer. Known notoriously in the West as monosodium glutamate, it is a common food additive, especially in fatty snacks, and is common fodder for urban legends about Chinese fare, eating too much of which is blamed for "syndromes." A side note: it's curious that Wong's Takeout and not Takeshi's Teriyaki gets the rap for this. Maybe Chinese cooks are heavy-handed?

Umami is a nice-sounding word, similar to *mm, yummy,* or *mommy.* It's easy to imagine that *umami* carries the cultural cachet and mystique of its motherland. The word has fallen into common usage among restaurateurs and foodies; at some high-end American eateries, there are special umami dishes. Whether produced by MSG or natural glutamate, it is a taste brought out through the interactions of various components, like chicken fat mixed with salt, shiitake mushrooms sautéed in soy sauce, or MSG-coated, fried cornmeal puffs. Descriptions resort to catch-phrases from scurrilous advertising: "hot and sat-isfying," "down-home comfort," "lip-smacking good." In Japan, the word is written on packaging for foods as far-flung as potato chips and the barley used in beer.

Umami is the noun form of *umai*, which means "delicious" or "tasty." It is said that Ikeda gave a name to, or engineered a concept for, a taste that isn't specific like salty, sweet, sour, or bit-ter. His invention is used all over the world to improve the fla-vor of foods, and there is even a scientific basis to it, something having to do with taste receptors and neurotransmitters. Just the right amount makes a normal dish the beau ideal, though it is difficult to gauge if the right amount of MSG has been used in comparison to the natural glutamic acid already present in many foods.

Eaters may have fooled themselves or been tricked into believing in MSG's magic. After all, MSG capitalizes on the "fat tooth" most people have. It gives to bland foods a meaty taste, as if there were animal protein in something like wheat crack-ers. In a way, MSG has become the taste of food in general. Without it, we aren't satisfied.

Would we evolve away from the need to answer this crav-ing were MSG not used to enhance almost every food product? "You can polish a turd," the saying goes, or spear it with a sprig of parsley. That's the sodium finish of *umami*, the mythical "fifth taste" of East Asia. In that region, where MSG is used in abun-dance, complaints of health problems are almost nonexistent. There may be something to the stereotype of different ethnici-ties being able to tolerate or prefer strong flavors.

❖

Lately I find myself wondering whether the food I'm eating contains MSG. It's become a habitual curiosity that sets me struggling to read the ingredients on food packages here in Japan.

The knowledge that MSG is extracted from cheap sources like molasses does not assuage my fears of its dangers. Why the lingering doubt, I don't know. But it's unnatural for MSG to occur in high concentrations. Maybe that's what I reason when I feel a little shaky after consuming an instant ramen and frozen gyoza dinner. Watchdog groups warn that MSG overexcites our synapses, maybe damages nerve receptors, and contributes to conditions like Parkinson's disease. "MSG" sounds like chemical death or overdose (maybe a byproduct of the acronym—think DDT or LSD).

Luckily, the myths about MSG's dangers have, for the most part, been proven unwarranted. After all, it is made simply by using water and salt to stabilize glutamic acid—a naturally occurring substance in cheese, tomatoes, and kombu seaweed, which is often in miso soup and is what led Ikeda to his research. *Umami* is the primary flavor sought, it seems, in Japanese cooking, and not spice or heat, as in Szechuan, Korean, or Thai cuisines. Without it Japanese food would be devoid of flavor: firm, salty, constant, yet delicate.

Delicious food here is not meant to excite or stimulate directly. It's more like enjoying the deep pleasure that comes of soaking in a hot bath, as opposed to a dive into a cold lake. The flavor of MSG also fits the general temperament of the Japanese. Not to get too anthropological, but the Japanese are not quick to anger, and are not prone to effusions of emotion. On the other hand, Koreans, who consume lots of red peppers and garlic, are said to be irascible, belligerent, and expressive.

What if fortune had dealt a different hand to Korea, and it arose as the predominant power in East Asia early in the twentieth century? Then, sometime in the late 1900s, a Korean scientist—to imagine a scenario similar to that which led to

Ikeda's discovery of umami—would have asked his wife what made her *kimchi chigae* (spicy Korean soup made with spiced, pickled cabbage, tofu, and usually pork) so delicious. She would have said it's because of the red peppers—it's the spicy kick that does it. This man would then have isolated capsaicin and packaged it as a flavor enhancer, and we might all be accustomed to eating spicy foods, and be sated once our bodies had released the ensuing endorphins. We would walk around feeling not calm and satisfied after dinner, but piqued and ready to brawl.

UMUNNEM | Kelechi Okere

It was already getting dark when we reached *nwannem* Baba's house in Umuneke. In Igboland, or Eastern Nigeria, people do not set out to visit one another when it is getting dark, because of dangerous roads. We wanted to personally invite Baba to my senior brother's upcoming traditional wedding and did not intend to stay long.

We parked out front next to a dying tree surrounded by a cluster of small cherry trees. Catching looks from neighbors and children playing in the sand, we walked around to the back of the house where Baba received guests. I was with *nwanne* my father, Uncle Titus, his son Nkemakolam who drove, and my two younger brothers *umunnem nwoke* Obi and Uche. Though Baba is my cousin, he is older than my Uncle Titus because his mother was my eldest aunt and Uncle Titus is the youngest among them. When Baba came out and saw us, he took our hands and greeted us excitedly. He called some of his neighbors to come and greet us. When they had come, he walked about hurriedly to bring us chairs to sit on outside and enjoy palm wine and bush meat with him. Baba's flock of chickens had learned to perch overnight on the tree branches above, so we were careful not to position our chairs directly under them.

"*Umunnem* welcome," Baba said, after we all sat down. "My heart feels good to see you. *Nwanne* is important *o!* Whoever has one is blessed and rich. And if you have many, your blessings are plenty."

He showed us the saucer of kola nuts and passed it around for everyone to see. When it had gone around and went back to him, he prayed over it and asked the youngest among us to break the kola nuts. "Look at Baba," Baba now addressed his neighbors, poking his chest with both hands. "Look at *umunne* Baba. Baba is a big man I tell you. There's no one around here that will dare insult me or look down on me knowing that I have people like them. Baba is a rich man, I tell you."

Baba was drunk, as we soon found out. He talked a lot, but the alcohol did not dilute the value of what he was saying. Rather, it enhanced his excitement over our visit. We had not seen him for a while, and he complained that Uncle Titus should have brought us much earlier, so that we would have had more time to talk. Uncle Titus purposefully planned our visit late because he knew Baba would have his wife cook for us and keep us for a long time if we came earlier.

Later, when we reached home and were sitting in the verandah of our bungalow laughing about Baba's drunkenness with my other cousins, *nwannem* Obi asked, "What does *nwanne* mean?" Obi did not know Igbo thoroughly because he was born in America. During our stay in Nigeria he often asked what this or that Igbo word meant. He wanted to learn to speak Igbo, so I took my time explaining things to him. Igbo can be a dense and beautiful language—which makes it more unsettling that it is dying.

"*Nwanne* means 'mother's child,'" I told him.

"I kinda figured it means relative or something like that, but wasn't sure of the whole meaning," he said. "But that's funny that the literal translation is 'mother's child' and I hear mommy use it to refer to our cousins."

"Well, you can use it to refer to any blood relative, but it's how you use it that makes a difference," I said to him. "Like if I want to say '*my* mother's child,' I'll say *nwannem* so-and-so. If I want to say my brother or sometimes male cousin, I'll say *nwannem nwoke,* and if I want to say my sister or sometimes female cousin, I'll say *nwannem nwanyi.* If I want to say my siblings or by extension, my blood relatives, I'll say *umunnem.*

"It sort of carries forward to the present the whole idea that we all came from one ancestral mother. So as long as you're a blood relative, you're my ancestral mother's child."

"That's cool," Obi said, and chuckled. Then he called out, "Hey *umunnem!*"

Everyone guffawed. "*Ehn* Obi you dey try, I beg," *nwannem nwanyi* Chioke said. "Keep it up."

When I remember that day with *nwannem* Baba and the time I had with *umunnem* in Nigeria when I visited, I long for home. I long for the late-night storytelling and laughing with them in the verandah, the palm wine and kola nuts in the morning with my Uncle Titus and sometimes Uncle Zeb. I am rich because *umunnem* are plenty in Nigeria.

UNKNOWABLE | Jillian Dungan

Idt seyms tu mee thad therza hole lot nlyfe thads unknowabl. Yz thee grazz iz greyne an yz thee skeye iz bloo. Yz thee cyrcl iz rownd ore yz thee fiar iz hawt ore yz thee waatr iz wett. Whych kame first thee chikin ore thee egg? Y doo peoples smyl went hay r haapie an froun went hay r saad? Theez thingz r unknowabl. Budt thaare r milyons uf thyngz thad r unknowabl. Iye thyink itz unknowabl y sum peepls r sooo bombastical. Idt seyms thad evrybuddiez bombasticl tu mee. Thay say thad iif iye doen unerstaand itz cuz thad iye em stooped. Thay say thad iye em unlearnabl iif iye thyink thad thyngaz iz unknowabl. Thay beeleev thad syence an pheelosophee can explayne thee world. An thad iif u look haard enuf then thee trooth wyll bee reeveeled. Thay beeleev thad evry qwestion has aanser. An itz jus cuz thay r bombasticl an thyink thad thay kno evrythyng. Thadz thee ownlee resin y thay r sew rood tu mee aall thee tym. Budt thei doen understand thad lotz uf stuhf nlyfe iz unknowabl. An itz unknowabl four themn tu. Itz ownlee thadt thay woent addmitit. Thayr tu prowd tu addmidit. An thay r tu scaird tu addmidit cuz iif thare r thyngz unknowabl then thay r naught

220

inn control. Thay caanut control whaat thay doen unerstaand. An sew thay pretend thad thay haav aall thee ansers an thadz thee wai idt iz supowsd tu b. Budt iye wiil naught preetend. Iye teel thee trooth, thad evry qwestion doen haav aanser. Iye em naught lyk theem. An maibee thad iz y thay r bombasticl tu mee, cuz thay doen unerstaand mee an thay r scaird. Sew iye say thad thayr thee wons thad r unlearnbl.

uR | Robin Hemley

Ur. City of Mes-Anni-Padda, succeeded by A-Anni-Padda, during whose reigns Ur fought constantly with other states of Mesopotamia. City of Abraham, who would sacrifice his own son if that's what God wanted. Ur-Jew. Ur-Muslim. Ur-Christian. Place the word *Ur* in front of any other word and watch as it causes the word to emit a charge, a pop, or sometimes a thin wisp of white smoke as the word folds into itself, becomes itself in its truest sense, reverts to something like a cousin, grows horns, or hoofs, loses its prehensile grip on modernity. *Ur-waistcoat. Ur-invasion. Ur-zebra. Ur-occupation. Ur-piano. Ur-insurgency.*

On a plain south of Nasiriyah, south of Babylon, near Baghdad, sit the ruins of Ur, like prophecy in reverse. Had the rulers of ancient Ur played Scrabble avidly, they might have chosen for the name of their ancient capital, Qz, worth twenty points as opposed to two. But the Ur board game, preceding all other board games, known as "Ur," contained only the letters *u* and *r*, as archaeologists have been able to piece together (literally) from "Ur" tiles uncovered in Ur. The object of "Ur" was to be original in the ontological sense: players placed tiles on the board until no space lay unclaimed, and every space formed one half of a binary, an "Ur" computer language, as it were.

The object of "Ur" in the larger sense was to make all space equal and indistinguishable—this game in itself was responsible for Ur's eventual disintegration as a culture, as the inhabitants of Ur, obsessed by the beauty of the infinite, left their great city vulnerable to successive invasions. In the same way as the great Northern Song Emperor of China, Huizang, perfected his calligraphy but neglected his army, the people of Ur, obsessed with style over substance, spent all their hours bent over a game that had no object and no end, and there remained deadlocked until their heads adorned the pikes of less artful enemies. Like some theologians, the late Romanian philosopher Mircea Eliade speculated in *Cosmos and History* that the great "Ur" players of Ur were never actually conquered, but simply became invisible as in some spell, like the child who closes his eyes. Unlike the child, perhaps they succeeded by the sheer concentration they applied to a game they never quite understood, a game without meaning or end. The raiders of Akkad found the city of Ur emptied of inhabitants, but full of signs of life (glowing hearths, food on the table, water flowing in the public baths). Perhaps, to this day, the players of "Ur" continue to play this aimless game in which all moves are equal, all moves therefore the first move, the "Ur-move," as it were, repeated infinitely under the shadow of the great ziggurat built to honor Nannar, god of the moon.

Perhaps when the ram's horn blows, the players of "Ur" praise the board, look up, then begin anew. One dumb syllable, dumb not as in "mute," but dumb as in "without comprehension." And by "comprehension," let us mean not "understanding," but "grasp." We cannot fully grasp Ur because it is the first, but also paradoxically the last. Ur. A pause. The final word uttered as the brain fizzles.

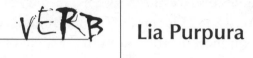 **Lia Purpura**

The life of the word consists in tensing and stretching itself toward a thousand connections, like the cut-up snake in the legend whose pieces search for each other in the dark.

—Bruno Schulz
(translated by Celina Wieniewska)

Run. Skate. Fly. Swim. The action words! "This is going to be fun," I remember thinking. And yes, back then the lively, kinesthetic world could be kept pretty simply in a flap-top box, marked with a nice black V. It was the kind of box you reached into, eyes closed, trusting, sure to get something good: *Row. Sow. Throw. Mow.* The contents of the box were familiar: *I* knew "slip!" *I* knew "dodge!" Spot *scampered.* Whiskers *lapped* milk from a bowl. Such easy finds on the subject-verb-object quizzes! Then things started dividing and growing: came forth the helping verb. The linking verb. Be-do-have-can-may-will-shall could be managed as a single breath-unit, a fit meditation for a rhythmic walk home, sotto voce and matched to stride, like "cross at the green, not in between."

224

The real complications began with echoes: I heard, early on, the *sea* in *see* which made that word an unfolding of riches. (Later I learned riches might be "seined" from the Seine: bouncing lamplight, scent of butter, smoked meat, wet leaves, cigarettes and—forgive me, this was my first time in Paris—such perfect and poised floating French trash.) *See* carried a translucing green tint and the sound of wavelets hitting the shore, each with a tiny white crest.

Nabokov had his synaesthetic swooning as a kid, and his pencil/sound/color configurations lived for him ever after. I had echoes in my verbs. *Corroborate* held *corrugate, collate, boric acid* (added for scouring if truth wasn't told when matching up facts). *Covet* held that weird tension between *covert* and *overt* (and once, in high school, *Corvette* layered in—oh, I wanted a red one. How clichéd! I thought I was better than that).

Sometimes when a verb's meanings crashed and swirled, I'd hear all the definitions at once, as in *Bound*: 1. rabbits leaping (innocent tinge). 2. corsets, ropes, etc. (not so innocent a tinge). 3. en route (Woody Guthrie, *Bound for Glory*; read-early-on romantic tinge). Even the word *verb* itself came with layers of sound: *herb, orb*, and most powerfully, *Erde* (for I could, at the time, pluck a few words from my mother's echt Grimms', before the heavy and leaning *Deutschrift* collapsed into decrees, proclamations—unreadable stories I had to imagine).

With so many echoes, traits, and suggestions, things came streaming. *Verb* got faster and faster.

It got slow and weird, too; *verb* still meant "action," but not as I knew it. Action widened, abstracted. *Contemplate* (I reasoned, I guessed on my test) was in the verb family. But distantly so. Where was the *action* in *contemplate*? As far as I knew (remember, I'm eight), *contemplate* was all stillness and quiet.

Then more happened: there were refractions. Things and actions rode one single rail. *Smattering* came—which could be a noun. (Traitor! Stay person-place-thing! Be rock-table-shoe unequivocally, please!) *Things* with *–ings?* Not fair. A smattering was all action—anyone could see that, on a wall, on a chair, it was jittery, splotchy, an anxious fat drip, undried where it fell, and perpetually sliding. *Roll* (v.) kept slipping into my mouth and was warm-golden-light, a morsel with weight/presence/butter. Or *roll*'s letters rose, puffed and settled into the (n.) breakfast they were, when they should've been doing (v.) somersault work.

So—a *roll* was a thing named for its action! Like a person named Skip, I supposed. And a Slurpee (purple, n.) was a badly disguised, badly spelled adjective. What was *role*, then, but a pacing and talking set of arm-waving gestures with weeping/imploring?

V! I marked down on my third-grade test. I knew from slash-heavy diagramming drills I was wrong—but all that slipping into another's skin, re-pitching the voice, distributing feelings. . . .

And yes, I was red-x assured: *role* was a *noun* (from the French, said my teacher, the paper—*le rôle*—containing the actor's part).

Thus it was learned: things would never stop moving.

VERSE | Albert Goldbarth

I'm remembering the farmer now. He's taken off his sword and belt and left them on a rock, and now he's laboring behind his sixteenth-century wooden plough (it may as well be ancient Greek, it's changed so little). As his stalwart horse is harnessed to the plough itself, the farmer is also—only a little more metaphorically—harnessed to his work.

They're going from right to left. Eventually they'll complete this row, and turn to do a row from left to right—then right to left again, and so forth, in the pattern that, indeed, is still described by a term from the ancient Greek: *boustrophedon*, "turning as the ox ploughs."

There are languages written and read that way, from left to right, then right to left, so down the page. English isn't one of them. It's interesting to think of the psychology, even the hand-eye physiology, of a culture that writes and reads its text in this ploughmanlike manner. Almost a science fiction writer's challenge: given a world of boustrophedon literature . . . what children's games and warfare and gods and weaver's designs and sexual shenanigans do we posit?

❖

Of course *boustrophedon* isn't the only writerly term that we can wring from this scene I'm loosely lifting out of Pieter Bruegel the Elder's *The Fall of Icarus*. When our farmer reaches the end of a row, he *verses*—that is, he turns, for that's what "verse" means. That's what a line of poetry does: it re-verses, consciously, from right to left. Another science fiction speculation: posit the difference in culture between the Planet of Poems and the Planet of Prose. What happy trade exists between the two, and what embargoes?

❖

"Lineation," I write on the board, and then "enjambment."

When I start to teach the "line break" to an undergraduate class, I give them a scraplet of my own creation, starting with the first line:

It is summer

at which I stop and ask what part of speech the word "summer" is. These days, some have no idea; but someone will finally say "noun." Then I continue:

It is summer
firewood we're burning now,
keeping us warm all winter.

Now? "It's an adjective" (these days, that takes many minutes). Right. You see? As the line breaks, so is our expectation of "summer"'s function broken. The line not only "turns," it kind of "turns around" and bites us. More than that, however, the line breaks . . . and our expectation breaks . . . just as we're given the implicit image of broken wood, and broken chemical bonds *inside* the burning wood . . . the language is mimetic of the action it's describing. And beyond even that . . . as we're given to see the wood's potential energy (stored up from June to December, let's say) made blazingly kinetic when the bonds break . . . so does "summer"'s being positioned at a breaking-point release a double energy (both adjective *and* noun) from it as well . . . we see it "verse," "turn" into two things simultaneously.

It isn't often as tough to write a poem as to plough a field. But Milton's *Paradise Lost* . . . that must have been a few fields. How many harvested milo-units (or wheat—or corn—or sorghum) go into Dante's midlife journey? We don't always sweat in our labor, we poets. And yet at the turn of the line, at least the *idea*, at least the *ghost* of an idea, of conscious and rigorous effort arises.

(In the attention traditional "light verse" often calls to the rhyme of its line breaks

> Or Moses or Napoleon or Cleopatra or King Midas,
> Or a man named Harris who is just getting over an
>   attack of tonsilidas
>   [from a poem by Ogden Nash]

it's the weightiest, heaviest-panting verse of all, and *not* the lightest.)

❖

Bruegel's painting is from 1588. It was as recent as 1520 that Magellan ploughed the ocean, turning his line around at the Cape. And even more recently, in 1543, Copernicus published his astronomical vision of turnings in turnings in turnings.

(We can say the act of circumnavigation of the planet is mimetic of the act of the planet's own travel.)

Bruegel himself was friends with Abraham Oertel (Ortelius), whose atlas of the world, *Theatrum Orbis Terrarum,* "took the maps compiled by various cartographers and redrew them using a uniform scale, bound them together in book form and sold them in a convenient volume" (Hagen).

(We can say that the maps—both sea and sky—for all of these newly-discovered turnings are really a body of literary criticism on verse.)

❖

The painting, of course, is only about that ploughman in the slyest of ways—or the shepherd amid his flock, or the fisherman busy casting his baited line. As you probably know, in a corner of the scene are the wildly waving legs that are all we can see of Icarus, who has fallen from his attempt to fly on artificial wings, and is drowning. He's like an asterisk down in that watery patch, reminding us for a moment of his grand myth and its baggage (Daedalus! Theseus! Minos! the Minotaur! the great soaring escape!) before our attention is drawn back to the larger, fuller figure.

That's the craftiness of Bruegel's point: the everyday has precedence here, as do the people who seem to find holistic satisfaction in their place in life. The myth has been "turned around," "turned on its head," "the tables have been turned" on the traditional tragic heroes and their lofty aspirations.

Which is to say, this is a version—a turning, a verse-ion—of the original myth.

❖

Ovid was one of the most well-known of the ancient poets in Bruegel's day, and the painter would have known Ovid's

Metamorphoses, where the story appears with the fisherman and the shepherd, just as the painting shows.

Metamorphoses: turnings, of one thing into another.

Bruegel's painting gets turned into a twentieth-century poem by Auden, then into a later twentieth-century poem by Randall Jarrell.

When we read them, we're tempted to turn back to Ovid's original. There, we're reminded of how Daedalus and Icarus were imprisoned on Minos's island (hence, their gloriously fatal attempt to escape on threaded wax-and-feathers wings) because of—if we trace the story back—the murder of Talos by Daedalus.

Talos, the apprentice who enraged his master Daedalus with jealousy: he had, for example, invented the potter's wheel. Turning, turning, turning.

Daedalus threw him off the roof of the Temple of Athena. "Murder," I said; but in the story, Athena takes pity on Talos and, mid-fall, she metamorphs him—turns him—into a bird.

This serves as a balance to the later (and unmediated) fall to death of Daedalus's son.

Of Talos, Ovid says that the bird he became is one that fears to fly too high; it merely skims the earth, and lays its eggs "not in trees or on cliffs," but "in brush on the ground."

And Bruegel has added a partridge here in the foreground, just the size of the far-off frantic legs of Icarus.

❖

It's on Minos's island that Daedalus constructs the fabled labyrinth, "his winding maze," in Horace Gregory's verse translation. Turning, turning, turning.

Theseus faces the dreaded Minotaur in the depths of those twists. They're much like halves, like doppelgängerish halves, of

231

a single being: the cultivated hero and his beast-self. (Much like Gilgamesh and Enkidu in the even earlier story.)

Ariadne, as we know, will help Theseus out of the maze with her ball of thread. That is, he'll "turn to her" for help.

And later on he'll abandon her; he'll "turn away" from her; and she, in her wrath, will "turn against him."

These are the tales that still beguile us, still tell us who we are, and why we stab one another with words (or worse), and why we dream of waking into nobler selves, and what we're like when our heart yearns or our conscience sleeps on the job. These are the tales that still get strutted out to shame us or inspire us, in rock and country-funk and hiphop, and paragraphed now onto blog upon blog, and squared into novels, and spooled into films.

But they started out in their true shapes, as verse.

❖

Who *doesn't* want, like Daedalus and Icarus, to fly?

To leave the earth?

To turn around the skies of the uni-verse!

An astronaut's orbit is surely one of the greatest of turnings; we could say, then, that the astronauts are (literally, if not linguistically) some of the greatest of versifiers.

In Elton John's song, the astronaut says: "And all this science I don't understand / It's just my job five days a week / A rocket man. A rocket man."

My job five days a week (well, two if I teach on a Tuesday-Thursday schedule) is talking about things just like this, to the handful of students who care, in the midst of the many thousands of students (and administrators and colleagues) who don't.

Most are here to seek money and status. Most are here, although they'd never phrase it this way, for vo-tech. Pre-law, pre-med, criminal justice, "information technology," aerospace engineering . . . jobs, jobs, jobs, jobs, jobs.

Sappho and Robert Bly are only unwanted diversions from that. Oh well.

If you look at its middle syllable, you might be led to think poetry was the central concern of a "university."

Sad to say, you'd be wrong.

In fact there are many who are averse to it.

VERY | Brock Clarke

I once knew a guy—a guy past the age where he could wear tight jeans but still wearing them, a guy with not enough hair in front to justify the ponytail in back—who asked a friend of mine out on a date. She was flustered by this, maybe because he was asking her out while I was standing right there next to her, and also maybe because she'd thought the guy was gay, and as everyone knows, when you're most flustered, you're also most likely to tell the truth, which was why my friend blurted out, "I thought you were gay."

"What?" the guy said, obviously offended, but trying to compose himself, stroking his ponytail, tugging at his jeans. "Why would you think that?"

"I don't know," my friend said, obviously embarrassed and wanting to get out of the conversation. "I just thought you were gay, that's all."

"Well, I'm not," the guy said.

"O.K.," she said. "I believe you."

"Good," the guy said. Then, trying to make sure my friend

really did believe him, he said something he shouldn't have: "I'm *very* heterosexual."

Is there a weaker, sadder, more futile word in the English language than *very*? Is there another word as fully guaranteed to prove the opposite of what its speaker or writer intends it to prove? Is there another word that so clearly states, on the speaker's or writer's behalf, "I'm not going to even *try* to find the right word," or "No matter how hard I try, I'm not going to find the right word"? Is there a less specific, less helpful, less necessary, less potent word in our vocabulary? There is not. The weatherman knows this when he tells us to bundle up because it's going to be *very* cold outside. The mother knows this when she tells her teenagers whom she's caught smoking out behind the garage *again* that she's *very* disappointed in them. Elmer Fudd knows this when he tells Bugs Bunny to be *vewy* quiet. Our students know this when they write, in their stories and by way of providing their characters the physical details we tell them their characters need in order to be characters, that so-and-so is *very* heavy, or *very* beautiful, or *very* statuesque. We all know this is an awful, lame word (John Cheever, in his story "The Wrysons," describes a group of rich people who travel up and down the eastern seaboard as being "*very* aquatic," and manages to employ [or deploy] the word as he did others—knowingly, beautifully; but it's dicey to try to write like Cheever, as I know *very* well to be true and maybe Cheever himself did, too). So why do we use this awful, lame word? Is it because we're too lazy to find the right word to describe the things that are most important to us? Or is it impossible to find the right word to describe those important things? When we say, "very," do we say, "I don't care"? Or do we say, "I care too much"?

I was watching my seven-year-old son read a book the other day—it was *The Clue of the Screeching Owl*, No. 41 in the Hardy Boys series. He was sitting on his bed, the book in front of his face, and didn't notice me standing in the doorway watching him. I must have stood there for five minutes, watching him read, watching him and watching him and falling deeper and deeper in love. What is it about seeing your children read that makes you love them so much, love them as much as you should love them all the time? I don't think it's only writers who feel this way. I don't think it's only readers who feel this way, either. I don't think it has anything to do with reading at all—after all, as far as spectator sports go, watching someone read is only slightly more exciting than watching someone play golf. Maybe it's easier to love a child at rest than a child in motion. Or maybe to watch a child reading is to watch a child not in any danger, a child you haven't put in peril, a child you haven't screwed up, or screwed up yet, or screwed up totally. Or maybe to watch a child who is unaware of you watching them is to watch something so perfect and unself-conscious that it is impossible to do anything but love them.

"What?" my son said. Because of course he'd noticed me standing there, and was now reading me the way he'd been reading the book a moment earlier, except he was reading me skeptically, suspecting, maybe, that I wanted something from him, whereas he'd been reading *The Clue of the Screeching Owl* with pleasure, and this, by the way, is the main reason we read: the people we love always want something from us, but the books we love do not want anything from us except that we read them.

"Nothing," I said. Because how could I tell him how I felt? How could I tell him I worry about him every second of every day except when he is reading? How could I tell him I would die if something bad happened to him, even something just a little bad that only caused me to die a little bit, and so as long as he kept reading and let me watch him do it I wouldn't have to die yet? How could I tell him that by reading he was giving me more time to love him? How do you say this kind of stuff to your son, or to anyone else for that matter? You don't; I didn't. Instead I said, "I love you very much."

My son looked at me over the top of his book. It was that parental look, full of disappointment. *"Very?"* his look seemed to say. "Is that the best you can do?" And then he returned to his book, which, presumably, hopefully, would do better.

wARRANT | Kathy Briccetti

I'm just speculating for a minute here; maybe the word *warrant* began during a war, probably a long-ago war like one during the Middle Ages. It could have begun as two words: *war ant,* a person who—like an ant laying its scented trail, its informational road between here and there, between home and food—crawled around from house to house delivering news of the war. *Where are the troops, where are more needed, when should they amass?* Serving a warrant back then might have meant, *Pack up, Hans, it's your turn to fight.* Maybe if a boy didn't go when called, a warrant for his arrest ensued.

But it's the verb form that intrigues me the most. It's not a verb that conjures images of mild or wild actions; the verb *to warrant* is a loosey-goosey abstraction that warrants further discussion. Warranting takes place only in one's head, and it's very subjective. It's a belief, an opinion, whether someone or something warrants someone or something else. As in:

That off-beat, somewhat controversial idea warrants action.

The bright, sunny day warranted light, flowing clothing.

His misogynistic attitude warrants reshaping.

The leak in the hull warranted a quick repair.

In my dictionary, which I have now opened, and which shows I was right about its Middle English origins, *warrant* sits between *warpwise* (a textile term that doesn't warrant many words here except that it means lengthwise, or with the warp of the fabric) and *warrantee*, which does warrant mention because of its root and its relationship to the word on the table here. A warrantee is not the same thing as a warranty—the agreement that allows one to return a broken dishwasher—it is a person to whom the warranty is made, the dishwasher's owner. It is the person who warrants a refund, or at least a free repair job if the appliance breaks within the warranty period.

If the word *warrant* doesn't work for you in your everyday conversations, if it sounds too highfalutin for your needs, my computer's thesaurus has a great list of user-friendly synonyms. Some of my favorites are: *merit, deserve, call for, affirm, certify,* and then three that sound like they could be Donald Duck's nephews: *secure, assure,* and *insure.*

I'm attracted to the word *warrant* because it suggests fairness and justice. And it's a powerful, no-nonsense word because, like a CEO, it can sanction, approve, and notarize. Like a defense attorney, it can explain, account for, offer grounds for, and be a reason or an argument for. It's the figurative book on which one swears one's honor, word, or promise, as in a court of law. There, it can attest or testify, even give testimonial to.

However, as in life, the presence of fairness is always disputable because the perception of fairness depends on who is passing judgment, and on what they believe warrants what. The subjectivity around what warrants what might even warrant some frustration, at times. And if people don't agree on what warrants what, they might get into an argument, which might start a war, and we'd be right back to the original Middle Ages meaning of the word, at least the original meaning according to my initial, unsubstantiated hypotheses.

WOOL | Daisy Fried

"Knitting?" says the midwife in the turquoise shoes when I tell where my hormones have taken me. "My grandmother used to make me sweaters to show how well she could knit. With epaulettes, fancy cables. It's female love and tradition." The handout she gives me advertises a cream that *reduces the appearance of cellulite*, $30 per 25 ml tube. That night, I dream my husband takes his yoga practice so far, he's required to hang all his weight from his balls. I am disturbed especially by the red thong underwear he wears.

"Strange dreams?" says the midwife with lopsided breasts. "Giving birth to a chimp or a slug?" The handout she gives me says, *Write how you'll feel if your baby comes out looking funny.* I dream a cop stops me for speeding, pulls me out of the car, flings me face down across the hood, rapes me.

I say I'm tired, can't even walk a half mile without sleeping an hour. "Husband being supportive?" says the youngest midwife. "Open mouth, open cervix. Yawn out and out in labor." She gives me *A Checklist for Birth Partners: 1. Listen. 2. Get involved.*

240

"Poor *thing!*" says my husband when I tell him my dreams. "No no!" I say. "I enjoyed it." We're sitting on a sun porch with coffee. Wool blanket overfurred with cat hairs around my feet. I knit the simplest of baby caps, *ultrabasic EZ infant rollbrim.* Not even wool: it's TLC Baby 100% acrylic. The wool is for his scarves. He doesn't wear them: the mud-colored one scratches his neck, the lichen-green sheds iridescent threads all over his black sweatshirts.

"Woolgathering?" he says. Goes over to potted cuttings clustered around the windows, rotates them, ruffs them up a little. He stole them from the botanic garden last fall, wonders which are doing well—improving—and which are failing. There's a moment when the two look almost the same.

Sun porch with coffee, 6:30 AM, the light having trouble getting wide open, and my eyes, and I yawn.

WRONG | John Shoptaw

I'm attached to my word the way I'm attached to my appendix: I'm not sure what it does, but I wouldn't want to do without it. I hear my word in my mind's ear ring out at me with a bright bronze gong, reverberating its exclamatory point: *Wrong!* Its final *ng*, stuck deep in the throat, resonates definitively, choking off any appeal. No word in English begins with this strangling sound (try *e-nglish* without the *e*). Then there's that opening *r*-sound, made in English with the tongue so righteously arched. Working backwards from *r* to *ng*, it's a wonder the swallowed word makes it out at all.

Which is not to forget that the opening *r* is spelled *wr*—a silent but crucial difference. The meaning of *wrong*, like *wring*, is rooted in turn and twist (I picture an unchanneled river). Almost any word you can think of beginning with *wr* (*wrangle, wrap, wrath, wreath, wrench, wrestle, wrinkle, wrist, writhe, write, wry*) means something contorted or bent. Whatever *wrong* is, it isn't *right*. Though they are antonyms, *wrong* and *right* don't toggle; two wrongs only make a wrong wronger. There are many ways to go wrong, some wrongdoings more wrongful than others. "He was her man," shrugs the refrain of "Frankie and Johnny," "but he done her wrong." Then there are the relatively innocent wrongs: the wrong answer, the wrong turn, the wrong number. Things too can go wrong, though it's not (we sometimes have to remind ourselves) their fault: something's wrong with this computer, this relationship, this answer. And in between lies the shifting mazy marshland of the socially or culturally wrong. One can say or do the wrong thing. Or do the right thing in the wrong way. One can wear one's coat or sweatshirt, accidentally or perversely, wrong side out. Note that we don't say wrong side in; the wrong side is the one found out.

My attachment to *wrong* feels physical to me, since I am left-handed. The other antonym of *right*—in the same listing boat as *wrong*—is *left*. Left-handers, neuroscience tells us, are literally wrongheaded. Whereas right-handers consistently process language in the left brain, left-handers are torn, and muddle through by crossing hemispheres—dyslexic, stammering, perpetually turned around. When not corrected, lefties write with the wrong hand, holding the pen wrong—hooking their wrists so as to pull their pen across the page, and leaving behind a scarcely followable trail of cramped characters. Sure, we can point to the inexplicably large number of like-handed presidents (Obama: "I'm a leftie, get used to it") and list the advantages of basking on both sides of the brain. Still, it's hard to shed the feeling of never being in the right.

Unlike *wring* or *wrinkle*, *wrong* seems to have taken on a figurative meaning from the beginning. As though the Old Norsemen and Norsewomen saw a crook in every creek. A figurative word, Aristotle tells us, is taken from its right and proper place and put into a wrong one. So I imagine him, perched on his barefoot tripod, shielding his eyes with his free hand from the shafts of the sun. Writing and speaking figuratively—with always the slight possibility that some new wrinkle of phrase might get off on the wrong foot into common parlance—is one of the most pleasant and pleasurable ways in which writers of either hand can indeed go wrong.

AFTERWORD: | A RUNAWAY VOWEL

brainsick, *adj*. Addleheaded; giddy.

—Samuel Johnson

Editor's note:
Any writer or editor of dictionaries will remain charmed and beset by the idea of what might have been written, and by what was missed. For a few years, I chased this book. I was chased by it. As I make my departure from it, I am convinced that I'm not alone. Other words have fled before me. Many another may flee after. So, farewell.

There are many letters in the alphabet, owned or traded among us for years, and yet one letter of the lot seems now to be missing. We feel the absence as a sadness, of course, but it's also a purgatorial inconvenience. Words in which the letter once resided are now heavy with its streaked ghost, a ransacking wildness. They have been rendered incomplete, and with an abruptness that can raise a bruise, or worse. How mortal the wound depends on the body of whichever leftover word.

Some words were once swayed by the old letter. Others were held together by it, a tree that surged. Such words can't ever be

245

themselves again, the experts tell us. Words less dependent have merely grown more veinous upon the letter's exit. These we can still mouth and taste and pen, though it's almost impossible meanwhile to avoid a beleaguered tone, a lullaby of chagrin sung to the remaining talk, the tongue.

True, a few surviving words seem to thrive without the vagrant, vagabonding *u* tucked into themselves. Words like those up and rattle, tumultuous with mantillas and bravura. After the pop and swish of performance, however, they too lie down depleted. For they have to teach themselves—or, we have to teach them—a style of eruption and the monotony of healing, again and again.

Conversation twists and alters without our favorite. We feel interrupted by fresh pauses in the language, and by animal complaints, the shifting organic. We may feel abandoned, but perhaps the letter, feeling still more abandoned, left us for a very good reason.

Don't words need our care? We scrub the outhouse, we paint a portrait of the day in suds, and in the same spirit, we claim—we "choose"—our words. The decision, though, seems stricken. We decide as we do led by our panic to say.

Yet the language is also talking to us; our language is talking *at* us. And sometimes we don't like that. A missing letter? A runaway vowel? We might be better off without it.

New words and syntax shall be constructed to make up for our loss. An appointed political committee will punish the fast-talking criminal wanderer, the bad partner, that *u*. We'll resubscribe to pride. Reassess all archaic expressions. Remove the "helping" verbs, who remind us, mistily, of the departed.

And we'll write with vim of other things.

Eventually, forgetfulness coats us. Public oratory shirks primeval moaning sounds. Lyrics thicken. Whistle that tune.

Once there was the sort of talk we'll probably never hear again. . . .

A child asks the mother: "But what did the letter sound like? Doesn't somebody, somewhere, still speak it?"

The father: "A historian in an out-of-the-way college town might have preserved it. But we can't tell what it meant to the people or precisely how they used it."

The child continues wondering, searches for it, looks up appropriate entries in the *World Book*, feels miffed, turns to a dictionary, and pages patiently through. But, there's nothing of the *u.*

The letter, rebuffing the culture, is gone, pounded afterwards by the readers. Only a very small aura tides. Not a shape on the page, not a bleat in the air.

The heraldry of thought is left the poorer for it. Signatures thin, evanescent, hemmed in by the unheard. "The problem is not to understand," someone is alleged to have proclaimed. "The problem is simply to *tell*. What can we bear if we don't manage to conserve our so very limited verbal resources?" Few hear her.

Startled by the *u*'s intransigence, the rest of the alphabet, as a matter of fact, has reconsidered its own prospects. They could all take off. *Do it!* But most of them just want a safe place to be and to be read. One renegade's enough. The other letters can't make a getaway, can't do what old what's-his-name did.

This conclusion worried the *q*, who was already feeling sensitive, linked by a longstanding association with the runaway. He feared that members of the alphabet would soon turn against him, accuse him of enabling the escape of the other fellow. Surely he had suspected something?

Besides, now he looked outdated. His profile suggested nefariously wrought hilts, dynasty, et cetera. However spindly, his nattiness recalled a bygone reign and the ambition to again attain it.

He kept his worries to himself.

I'll make it to hypotenuse! Someday, I'll even make it to Carthage. Then on to the Bodhisattva of Compassion, draped in swelling and cumbersome vine. Though nearly alone in a world of fractious, mettlesome words, the *q* vowed to learn what he could of the past and present.

Some of us especially enjoy his whiplash calligraphic do-si-dos. With a guarded nostalgia, we trace his gaudy hippocampus shape on our notepads. He plays and flinches in the ear, until we eavesdrop.

—Molly McQuade

CONTRIBUTOR NOTES

Meena Alexander is the author of books including *The Shock of Arrival: Reflections on Postcolonial Experience, Stone Roots,* and *Quickly Changing River.* She has been a visiting lecturer at the Sorbonne and a writer-in-residence at the Center for American Culture Studies at Columbia University. She is Distinguished Professor of English at the City University of New York.

Ted Anton is a journalist and nonfiction writer whose books include *Eros, Magic, and the Murder of Professor Culianu.* He teaches literary nonfiction at DePaul University in Chicago. The subject of his current research is longevity genes.

Priscilla Becker's first book of poems, *Internal West* (2003), won *The Paris Review* book prize. Her poetry has appeared widely in journals and in the *Swallow Anthology of New American Poets*; her reviews in *The Nation* and the *New York Sun*; and her essays in *Cabinet* and elsewhere. Her second book of poetry, *Stories That Listen,* is forthcoming.

April Bernard, poet and novelist, is the author most recently of *Romanticism* (poems). Her other books include the poetry volumes *Swan Electric, Psalms,* and *Blackbird Bye Bye,* and the novel *Pirate Jenny.* She is the Director of Creative Writing at Skidmore College.

Susan Bernofsky has translated four books by the great Swiss-German modernist author Robert Walser, as well as novels by Jenny Erpenbeck, Yoko Tawada, Hermann Hesse, and others. Currently she is writing two books: a biography of Robert Walser and a novel set in her hometown, New Orleans.

Star Black was raised in Coronado, California; Washington, DC; and Hawaii. Her poems have appeared in *The Penguin Book of the Sonnet, 110 Stories: New York Writes After September 11,* and *Best American Erotic Poems from 1800 to the Present.* An exhibition of her art, "A Poet's Eye for Collage," was held at Poets House in New York City. She is the co-founder of the KGB Bar Poetry Reading Series.

Kathy Briccetti's memoir, *Blood Strangers,* was published in May 2010 by Heyday Books. Her awards include a Vermont Studio Center residency. She can be reached through her website: www.kathybriccetti.com.

Joel Brouwer is the author of three books of poems: *Exactly What Happened, Centuries,* and *And So.* He teaches at the University of Alabama.

Brock Clarke is the author of four books of fiction, most recently the novel *An Arsonist's Guide to Writers' Homes in New England.* His fiction and nonfiction have appeared in *The Believer, New England Review, One Story, Virginia Quarterly Review, Ninth Letter, Georgia Review, Southern Review,* and in the *Pushcart Prize* and *New Stories from the South* anthologies. He teaches at Bowdoin College.

Joan Connor is the author of three story collections: *Here on Old Route 7, We Who Live Apart,* and *History Lessons.* Her collection of essays, *The World Before Mirrors,* won the River Teeth award. She teaches at Ohio University and in the low-residency MFA program at Fairfield University.

William Corbett is a poet, memoirist, and art critic living in Boston. He teaches writing at MIT, is on the advisory board of Manhattan's CUE Art Foundation, and directs the small press Pressed Wafer. Recent books are *Poems on Occasion* (Pressed Wafer) and *Opening Day* (Hanging Loose Press).

Katherine DeLorenzo is a writer in New York. She teaches at Hunter College.

Jane Delury's short stories have appeared in *Prairie Schooner, StoryQuarterly,* and *The Sun.* A graduate of the Johns Hopkins Writing Seminars, she is a writer-in-residence in the University of Baltimore's MFA program in Creative Writing & Publishing Arts.

Jillian Dungan is a young writer from Illinois.

Annie Finch is author or editor of fifteen books of poetry, translation, and criticism, most recently *Among the Goddesses.* Her work was short-listed for the ForeWord Book of the Year Award in poetry and won the Fitzgerald Award. She directs Stonecoast, the low-residency MFA program of the University of Southern Maine.

Daisy Fried is the author of *My Brother Is Getting Arrested Again*, a finalist for the National Book Critics Circle Award, and *She Didn't Mean to Do It*, which won the Agnes Lynch Starrett Prize. A recent Guggenheim Fellow, she lives in Philadelphia.

Daina Lyn Galante, a recipient of the Edna N. Herzberg Award, is a young writer in New Jersey. This is her first publication. She believes that wit will conquer all.

Forrest Gander is the author of many books of poetry (e.g., *Science & Steepleflower*), as well as novels, essays, and translations. A recipient of grants and awards from the National Endowment for the Arts, the Guggenheim Foundation, and the Whiting Foundation, among others, he is a professor of English and Comparative Literature at Brown University.

Cynthia Gaver is a teacher and writer in Maryland.

Two of **Albert Goldbarth**'s two dozen books of poetry, *Saving Lives* and *Heaven and Earth*, received the National Book Critics Circle Award. His collections of essays include *A Symphony of Souls* and *Great Topics of the World*. Goldbarth teaches at Wichita State University.

Siobhan Gordon is a young writer in New York City.

Robin Hemley's books include both nonfiction (*Nola: A Memoir*; *Invented Eden*) and fiction (*The Last Studebaker*). He directs the nonfiction writing program at the University of Iowa.

Brenda Hillman teaches at Saint Mary's College of California, where she is Olivia Filippi Professor of Poetry. She is the author of eight collections of poetry, all published by Wesleyan University Press, the most recent of which is *Practical Water*.

Maggie Hivnor grew up in New York City; her work has appeared in

251

Carolina Quarterly and *Journal of Scholarly Publishing.* She lives with her family and other animals in Hyde Park, Chicago, where she is paperback editor at the University of Chicago Press.

Andrew Hudgins' most recent book is *Shut Up, You're Fine: Poems for Very, Very Bad Children,* with illustrations by Barry Moser. His next book, *American Rendering: New and Selected Poems,* is scheduled for release in 2010 from Houghton Mifflin Harcourt. He teaches at Ohio State University.

Jayson Iwen has lived in Guatemala, Ireland, and Lebanon, where he taught at the American University of Beirut. His books include *A Momentary Jokebook* and *Six Trips in Two Directions.*

Laura Jacobs writes for *Vanity Fair* and is the dance critic for *New Criterion.* Her second novel, *The Bird Catcher,* was published by St. Martin's Press in 2009.

Katherine Karlin's fiction has been anthologized in the *Pushcart Prize* series and in *New Stories from the South,* and has also appeared in *ZYZZYVA, Alaska Quarterly Review, One Story, North American Review,* and elsewhere. She teaches creative writing at Kansas State University.

Vincent Katz is a poet, critic, and translator. The author of ten volumes of verse, Katz won the 2005 National Translation Award for his translations from Latin of *The Complete Elegies of Sextus Propertius* (Princeton). He is the publisher of *Vanitas* magazine and Libellum Books.

Megan Kossiakoff is a human rights lawyer living currently in Kosovo. Her writing has lately focused on developing creative legal theories for protecting religious and cultural heritage in a post-conflict environment. She is still obsessed with finding a good pen.

Marilyn Krysl's writing has appeared in *The Atlantic, The New Republic, Best American Short Stories, O. Henry Prize Stories,* and the *Pushcart Prize* series. Her fourth collection of stories, *Dinner with Osama,* won the Richard Sullivan Prize and *ForeWord Magazine*'s bronze prize for best story collection. *Swear the Burning Vow: Selected and New Poems,* was published in 2009 by Ghost Road Press.

Dan Machlin's most recent book of poems is *Dear Body* (Ugly Duckling Press), which received a CLMP/Jerome Foundation "Face Out" grant for emerging writers. His poems and reviews have appeared widely. He is the founder and senior editor of Futurepoem Books, an award-winning publisher of innovative literature, and is a former curator of the Segue Reading Series in New York City.

Elizabeth Macklin is the author of *A Woman Kneeling in the Big City* and *You've Just Been Told* and the translator of Basque poet Kirmen Uribe's *Meanwhile Take My Hand*. In 1999, an Amy Lowell Poetry Travelling Scholarship led to her studying Euskara and learning the word *lasai*.

Lee Martin is the author of *The Bright Forever*, a finalist for the 2006 Pulitzer Prize in fiction; *River of Heaven*; *Quakertown*; *Turning Bones*; *From Our House*; and *The Least You Need to Know*. He teaches in the MFA program at Ohio State University.

Michael Martone was born in Fort Wayne, Indiana, and he is happy that, now, his computer actually counts the number of words allotted to tell his life story, like robotic Fates, measuring out the length of the line, there, in the bottom of the window, cutting him off at

Erin McGraw is the author of five books of fiction including, most recently, *The Seamstress of Hollywood Boulevard*. She teaches at Ohio State University.

Maureen N. McLane is the author of two books of poems, *World Enough* and *Same Life*, both published by Farrar, Straus and Giroux. She has also published two books of literary criticism with Cambridge University Press: *Balladeering, Minstrelsy, and the Making of British Romantic Poetry* and *Romanticism and the Human Sciences*. "Kankedort" will appear in her forthcoming volume, *My Poets*.

Albert Mobilio is the recipient of a Whiting Writers' Award and the National Book Critics Circle Award for book reviewing. His collections of poetry include *Bendable Siege*, *The Geographics*, *Me with Animal Towering*, and *Letters from Mayhem*. He is an assistant professor of literary studies at the New School's Eugene Lang College and an editor of *Bookforum*.

Rusty Morrison's *the true keeps calm biding its story* won the Academy of American Poets' James Laughlin Award, the Northern California Book Award, and Ahsahta's Sawtooth Prize. *Whethering* won the Colorado Prize for Poetry. Her criticism and poems have appeared in *APR, Boston Review, Chicago Review,* and *Denver Quarterly.* She is co-publisher of Omnidawn.

Thylias Moss's volumes of poetry include *Slave Moth* and *Small Congregations: New and Selected Poems.* She has also published plays and a memoir, *Tale of a Sky-Blue Dress.* She has received a MacArthur Fellowship, a Guggenheim Fellowship, and a Whiting Award, among others. She teaches at the University of Michigan.

Dan Moyer is a young writer in New Jersey.

Robert Mueller, an independent scholar, has contributed poems and essays to *First Intensity, American Letters & Commentary, Jacket, Ink Node, Spinozablue,* and other publications. He maintains a critical preference for Barbara Guest while searching far afield among past literatures, languages, and aesthetic disciplines, as well as unplanned varieties of American innovation.

Mark Noonan is founding editor of the *Columbia Journal of American Studies* and teaches English at New York City College of Technology, CUNY. He is coeditor of *The Place Where We Dwell: Reading and Writing About New York City,* and the author of *Reading The Century Illustrated Monthly Magazine: American Literature and Culture, 1870–1893* (Kent State University Press, 2010).

Kelechi Okere was born in Nigeria in 1980 to Igbo parents. He immigrated to the U.S. in 1992 to rejoin his parents, who had left Nigeria in 1982. He received his education at Rutgers University and lives in New Jersey. This is his first publication in a book.

Eric Ormsby is the author of six collections of poetry, including *For a Modest God* (Grove Press). His work has appeared in journals in Britain, Canada, and the U.S. and is included in *The Norton Anthology of Poetry.* A new selection, *The Baboons of Hada,* will appear in 2011 from Carcanet. He lives in London.

Lia Purpura's *On Looking* was a National Book Critics Circle Award finalist in nonfiction. Her book of poems, *King Baby*, won the Beatrice Hawley Award. Recent work has appeared in *The New Yorker, The New Republic, Agni,* and *The Paris Review.* An NEA and Fulbright recipient, she is writer in residence at Loyola University in Baltimore.

Lawrence Raab is the author of six collections of poetry, including *The Probable World* (Penguin, 2000), *What We Don't Know About Each Other* (Penguin, 1993), a winner of the National Poetry Series and a finalist for the National Book Award, and *Visible Signs: New and Selected Poems* (Penguin, 2003). He has also published a chapbook of collaborative poems with Stephen Dunn, *Winter at the Caspian Sea* (Palanquin Press, 1999). He teaches literature and writing at Williams College.

Wendy Rawlings is the author of a novel, *The Agnostics,* and a collection of short stories, *Come Back Irish.* Her fiction and nonfiction have appeared in *The Atlantic, Tin House, Indiana Review, Southern Review, AGNI, Colorado Review,* and other magazines. She teaches in the MFA program at the University of Alabama.

Srikanth Reddy is the author of *Facts for Visitors.* His next collection of poetry, *Voyager,* is forthcoming from the University of California Press in 2011. A graduate of the Iowa Writers Workshop and the PhD program in English literature at Harvard, Reddy is currently an assistant professor at the University of Chicago.

John Rodriguez is a Bronx poet and scholar. He earned a PhD in English from the Graduate Center at the City University of New York. His writing has appeared in the anthologies *Hokum, Bum Rush the Page,* and *Home Girls Make Some Noise.* He tries to work things out every other weekend at a time.

Mimi Schwartz is the author of five books, including *Good Neighbors, Bad Times—Echoes of My Father's German Village,* which received the ForeWord Book of the Year Award in memoir for 2008. Her essays have appeared in the *New York Times, Tikkun, Creative Nonfiction,* and elsewhere.

Yong-Woong Shin is a proofreader in New York City and a graduate of the University of Washington and Rutgers University. For two years he lived in Japan. His parents immigrated from Korea; he was born and raised in the United States.

John Shoptaw teaches poetry reading and writing at the University of California, Berkeley. He wrote the libretto for the opera *Our American Cousin*, composed by Eric Sawyer, which is available on CD (BMOP/sound).

Peggy Shumaker's new book of poems is *Gnawed Bones* (Red Hen Press). Her memoir, *Just Breathe Normally*, is now available in paperback from Bison Books (University of Nebraska Press). She teaches in the Rainier Writing Workshop MFA Program and can be reached at www.peggyshumaker.com.

Karen Stolz received an MFA from the Iowa Writers' Workshop. Her novel *World of Pies* was published in six foreign countries, as well as in the U.S., and was a *School Library Journal* Best Adult Book for Young Adults. Stolz is also the author of *Fanny and Sue*. She teaches at Pittsburg State University.

Mary Swander is the poet laureate of Iowa. Her books include poetry (*Girls on the Roof*); memoir (*The Desert Pilgrim*, a Barnes & Noble Discover Great New Writers selection); and *Parsnips in the Snow*. She teaches at Iowa State University, plays the banjo, and raises goats.

Cole Swensen is the author of twelve books of poetry, most recently *Ours* (University of California Press). Among her other books were a finalist for the National Book Award and winners of the Iowa Poetry Prize, the San Francisco State Poetry Center Book Award, and the National Poetry Series.

Arthur Sze is the author of nine books of poetry, including *The Ginkgo Light* (2009) and *Quipu* (2005) from Copper Canyon Press. He is also the editor of *Chinese Writers on Writing*, forthcoming in 2010 from Trinity University Press.

John Taggart is a poet and critic whose books include *Dehiscence*,

Standing Wave, and *Pastorelles*. His prose includes *Remaining in Light: Ant Meditations on a Painting by Edward Hopper* and *Songs of Degrees: Essays on Contemporary Poetry and Poetics*.

Nathaniel Taylor is a young writer and photographer from the Washington, DC, area.

Richard Terrill is the author of a collection of poems, *Coming Late to Rachmaninoff*, winner of the Minnesota Book Award, and two books of creative nonfiction, *Fakebook: Improvisations on a Journey Back to Jazz* and *Saturday Night in Baoding: A China Memoir*, winner of the Associated Writing Programs Award.

Willett Thomas earned her MA in creative writing from Johns Hopkins. She has received artist's fellowships from Blue Mountain Center and the Millay Colony. She was selected as a Mid-Atlantic Arts Foundation Fellow for the District of Columbia. She is the recipient of the 2008 Maureen Egen Writers Exchange Award for fiction.

Rachel Toor teaches in the MFA program in Eastern Washington University in Spokane. Her recent book is *Personal Record: A Love Affair with Running*. She writes a monthly column for the *Chronicle of Higher Education* and a bimonthly column for *Running Times*. She can be reached at www.racheltoor.com.

Katherine Vaz was a Briggs-Copeland Fellow in Fiction at Harvard University and a 2006 Fellow of the Radcliffe Institute for Advanced Study. She has published two novels: *Saudade*, and *Mariana*, which has appeared in six languages and was picked by the Library of Congress as one of the Top Thirty International Books of 1998. Her collection *Fado & Other Stories* won the Drue Heinz Literature Prize, and *Our Lady of the Artichokes* won a Prairie Schooner Book Prize.

Eleanor Wilner has published six books of poetry, most recently *The Girl with Bees in Her Hair* (Copper Canyon Press), *Reversing the Spell: New and Selected Poems* (Copper Canyon), and *Otherwise* (University of Chicago Press).

AUTHOR INDEX

Alexander, Meena, *ammavide,* 18
Anton, Ted, *riff,* 168
Becker, Priscilla, *personal,* 157
Bernard, April, *sweet,* 197
Bernofsky, Susan, *dämmerung,* 52
Black, Star, *bitchin',* 26
Briccetti, Kathy, *warrant,* 238
Brouwer, Joel, *a,* 9
Clarke, Brock, *very,* 234
Connor, Joan, *lilac,* 136
Corbett, William, *gray,* 103
DeLorenzo, Katherine, *blog,* 27
Delury, Jane, *negligee,* 147
Dungan, Jillian, *unknowable,* 220
Finch, Annie, *felt,* 77
Fried, Daisy, *wool,* 240
Galante, Daina Lyn, *eek,* 72
Gander, Forrest, *dehiscence,* 60
Gaver, Cynthia, *I,* 119
Goldbarth, Albert, *verse,* 227
Gordon, Siobhan, *floccinaucinihilipilification,* 89
Hemley, Robin, *ur,* 222
Hillman, Brenda, *as,* 20
Hivnor, Maggie, *half-light,* 105
Hudgins, Andrew, *nut,* 150
Iwen, Jayson, *interesting,* 123
Jacobs, Laura, *ardor,* 19
Karlin, Katherine, *corn,* 43
Katz, Vincent, *florere,* 91
Kossiakoff, Megan, *ickybicky,* 122
Krysl, Marilyn, *filthy,* 82
Machlin, Dan, *invisible,* 126
Macklin, Elizabeth, *lasai,* 134
Martin, Lee, *colander,* 32
Martone, Michael, *thermostat,* 202

McGraw, Erin, *darb,* 54
McLane, Maureen N., *kankedort,* 129
McQuade, Molly, *doom,* 65
Mobilio, Albert, *baffle,* 23
Morrison, Rusty, *echo,* 67
Moss, Thylias, *six-pack,* 170
Moyer, Dan, *crash,* 47
Mueller, Robert, *still,* 193
Noonan, Mark, *prefer,* 162
Okere, Kelechi, *umunnem,* 217
Ormsby, Eric, *or,* 152
Purpura, Lia, *verb,* 224
Raab, Lawrence, *sweetie,* 199
Rawlings, Wendy, *fiasco,* 78
Reddy, Srikanth, *fact,* 76
Rodriguez, John, *hope,* 109
Schwartz, Mimi, *forget,* 97
Shin, Yong-Woong, *umami,* 213
Shoptaw, John, *wrong,* 242
Shumaker, Peggy, *dive,* 62
Stolz, Karen, *careen,* 30
Swander, Mary, *topsoil,* 204
Swensen, Cole, *solmizate,* 191
Sze, Arthur, *quipu,* 165
Taggart, John, *subitane,* 195
Taylor, Nathaniel, *pants,* 155
Terrill, Richard, *dassn't,* 56
Thomas, Willett, *midnight,* 145
Toor, Rachel, *H.O.T.T.,* 112
Vaz, Katherine, *eye,* 74
Wilner, Eleanor, *line,* 142

MOLLY MCQUADE has worked as an editor of books, journals, and magazines for the Great Books Foundation, *Publishers Weekly,* Wesleyan University Press, *TriQuarterly, Parnassus, Chicago Review,* and others. Her prose or poetry has appeared in *Yale Review,* the *New Criterion,* the *Washington Post,* the *Village Voice,* the *Atlantic,* the *American Scholar, Daedalus, Literary Imagination,* the *Threepenny Review,* the *Paris Review,* and more. McQuade writes two columns for the American Library Association, and served previously as a columnist for *Hungry Mind Review.* She has received fellowships or awards from the National Council of Teachers of English, the Pew Charitable Trusts, and the New York Foundation for the Arts. Among her books are a collection of her essays, *Stealing Glimpses* (Sarabande Books), and *An Unsentimental Education* (University of Chicago Press). A frequent panelist and presenter at conferences including the AWP, the MLA, and elsewhere, she has taught literature and writing at the School of the Art Institute of Chicago, Johns Hopkins, the Unterberg Center, and other venues. She blogs for PEN.